Identifying the Developmentally Delayed Child

Identifying the Developmentally Delayed Child

Selected Papers of the Third International Conference
on Early Identification of Children
Who Are Developmentally "At Risk"
Teton Village, Wyoming

Edited by

Nicholas J. Anastasiow, Ph.D.
Hunter College
New York, New York
William K. Frankenburg, M.D.
and
Alma W. Fandal
John F. Kennedy Child Development Center
University of Colorado Health Sciences Center
Denver, Colorado

University Park Press
Baltimore

UNIVERSITY PARK PRESS
International Publishers in Science, Medicine, and Education
300 North Charles Street
Baltimore, Maryland 21201

Copyright © 1982 by University Park Press

Composed by Maryland Composition Company, Inc.

Manufactured in the United States of America by the Maple Press Company

Library of Congress Cataloging in Publication Data

International Conference on Early Identification of Children Who Are
Developmentally "At Risk" (3rd : 1980 : Teton Village, Wyo.)
Identifying the developmentally delayed child.

Includes index.
1. Child development—Testing—Congresses. 2. Medical screening—Congresses.
3. Child development deviations—Diagnosis—Congresses. I. Anastasiow, Nicholas
J. II. Frankenburg, William K. III. Fandal, Alma W. IV. Title.
[DNLM: 1. Child development disorders—Diagnosis—Congresses. W3 IN172P 3rd
1980i / WS 350.6 I59 1980i]

RJ51.D48I57   1980   618'92'8588075   81-21838
ISBN 0-8391-1729-9   AACR2

Contents

SECTION III
COMPREHENSIVE IDENTIFICATION PROGRAMS

Contributors

Nicholas J. Anastasiow, Ph.D. *
Professor, Special Education
Hunter College
440 East 26th Street, 7th floor
New York, New York 10010   USA

Robert H. Bradley, Ph.D. *
Center for Child Development
  and Education
University of Arkansas at Little Rock
33rd and University
Little Rock, Arkansas 72204   USA

Jeanne Brooks-Gunn, Ph.D.
Educational Testing Service
Rosedale Road
Princeton, New Jersey 08541   USA

Yueh-mei Chu
Shanghai No. 6 People's Hospital
Shanghai, PEOPLE'S REPUBLIC
  OF CHINA

Dr. A. T. M. Cools *
Algemeen Direkteur
Instituut Voor Geestelijk
  Gehandicapten
Emeroord
Zandheuvelweg 4-3744 MN Baarn
The NETHERLANDS

Cecilia E. Coons, M.A. *
John F. Kennedy Child Development
  Center
University of Colorado Health Sciences
  Center
4200 East Ninth Avenue, C234
Denver, Colorado 80262   USA

Margaret Cox, M.D. *
The Doctor Charles A. Janeway Child
  Health Centre
Newfoundland Drive
St. John's, Newfoundland A1A 1R8
CANADA

Jan L. Culbertson, Ph.D. *
Assistant Professor of Pediatrics
Vanderbilt University
Division of Child Development
Department of Pediatrics
Nashville, Tennessee 37232   USA

Craig Edelbrock, Ph.D. *
Pittsburgh Child Guidance Center
201 DeSoto Street
Pittsburgh, Pennsylvania 15213   USA

Bernice S. L. Eu, M.B.B.S. * *
Mothers' and Babies' Health
  Association
285-295 So. Terrace
Adelaide, SOUTH AUSTRALIA 5000

Alma W. Fandal *
John F. Kennedy Child Development
  Center
University of Colorado Health Sciences
  Center
4200 East Ninth Avenue, C234
Denver, Colorado 80262   USA

Peggy C. Ferry, M.D. *
Department of Pediatrics
University of Arizona Health Sciences
  Center
Tucson, Arizona 85724   USA

William K. Frankenburg, M.D.*
Director, John F. Kennedy Child
  Development Center
University of Colorado Health Sciences
  Center
4200 East Ninth Avenue, C234
Denver, Colorado 80262   USA

Elizabeth C. Gay, M.A.*
John F. Kennedy Child Development
  Center
University of Colorado Health Sciences
  Center
4200 East Ninth Avenue, C234
Denver, Colorado 80262   USA

Dr. J. M. A. Hermanns*
R. U. Utrecht
IPAW, Vakgroep Ontwikkeling-
  psychologie
Heidelberglaan 1
3584 CS Utrecht
HOLLAND

Harold Ireton, Ph.D.*
Department of Family Practice and
  Community Health
University of Minnesota Health
  Sciences Center
Box 381—Mayo Memorial Building
420 Delaware Street, SE
Minneapolis, Minnesota 55455   USA

Jose R. Jordan, M.D., D.Sc.*
Ministrio de Salud Publica
Consejo Cientifico
Calle 23, No. 201, 4to Piso
Vedado - LaHabana
CUBA

Cynthia Ker*
John F. Kennedy Child Development
  Center
University of Colorado Health Sciences
  Center
4200 East Ninth Avenue, C234
Denver, Colorado 80262   USA

Xing-yuan Koo, M.D.
Shanghai First Medical College
Shanghai, PEOPLE'S REPUBLIC
  OF CHINA

Dianne L. Lefly, M.A.*
John F. Kennedy Child Development
  Center
University of Colorado Health Sciences
  Center
4200 East Ninth Avenue, C234
Denver, Colorado 80262   USA

Michael Lewis, Ph.D.*
Educational Testing Service
Rosedale Road
Princeton, New Jersey 08541   USA

Melvin D. Levine, M.D.
Associate Professor, Harvard Medical
  School
Chief, Ambulatory Pediatrics
Children's Hospital Medical Center
300 Longwood Avenue
Boston, Massachusetts 02115   USA

Robert Lichtenstein, Ph.D.**
28 Sidlaw Road #3
Brighton, Massachusetts 02135   USA

Robert B. McCall, Ph.D.*
Boys Town Center for the Study of
  Youth Development
Boys Town, Nebraska 68010   USA

Samuel J. Meisels, Ed.D.
Associate Professor and Chairman of
  Special Education
University of Michigan
3112 School of Education Building
Ann Arbor, Michigan 48109   USA

Tore Mellbin, M.D.
Department of Pediatrics
University Hospital
S-75014 Uppsala 14
SWEDEN

Donald E. Pierson, Ph.D.*
Director, Brookline Early Education
  Project
287 Kent Street
Brookline, Massachusetts 02146   USA

Potluri B. Rao, M.D.
Rockford Regional Perinatal Center
Rockford Memorial Hospital
2400 North Rockton Avenue
Rockford, Illinois 61101   USA

Herta M. Schrom, M.D.
Rockford Regional Perinatal Center
Rockford Memorial Hospital
2400 North Rockton Avenue
Rockford, Illinois 61101   USA

Marian Sigman, Ph.D.
Department of Psychiatry School of
    Medicine
Neuropsychiatric Institute
Center for Health Sciences
760 Westwood Plaza
Los Angeles, California 90021   USA

Gerald F. Staub, M.D.
Rockford Regional Perinatal Center
Rockford Memorial Hospital
2400 North Rockton Avenue
Rockford, Illinois 61101   USA

Claes Sundelin, M.D.*
Chief Officer of Child Health
Department of Pediatrics
University Hospital
S-75014 Uppsala 14
SWEDEN

Cheih Sung, M.D., Yueh-Mei Chu,
    and Xing Yuan Koo**
Shanghai No. 6 People's Hospital
Shanghai, PEOPLE'S REPUBLIC
    OF CHINA

John F. Sweet, Jr., Ed.D.,* Gerald
    Staub, Herta Schrom, and
    Potluri Rao**
Central Wisconsin Center
317 Knutson
Madison, Wisconsin 53704   USA

Terrence Tivnan, Ph.D.
Associate Professor of Education
Harvard Graduate School of Education
Larsen Hall 417
Appian Way
Cambridge, Massachusetts 02138   USA

Reiko Ueda, M. Litt, D.M.S.,* and
    Seiko Yokozawa**
Department of Maternal and
    Child Health
University of Tokyo
School of Health Sciences
Faculty of Medicine
Hongo, Bunkyo-su, Tokyo 113
JAPAN

Judy A. Ungerer, Ph.D. and
    Marian Siginan**
Department of Psychiatry School of
    Medicine
Neuropsychiatric Institute
Center for Health Sciences
760 Westwood Plaza
Los Angeles, California 90021   USA

Jean-Claude Vuille, M.D.
Department of Pediatrics
University Hospital
S-75014 Uppsala 14
SWEDEN

Ole Wasz-Höckert, M.D.**
Professor of Pediatrics
Children's Hospital
University of Helsinki
Stenbackstreet 11
SF-00290 Helsinki 29
FINLAND

Professor Dr. Med. Victor Weidtman**
Direktor
Des Instituts Für Medizinische Doku-
    mentation and Statistik
Der Universitat Zü Köln
Joseph-Stelzmann-Str. 9
5000 Köln 41
WEST GERMANY

Emmy E. Werner, Ph.D.*
Department of Developmental
    Psychology
University of California at Davis
Davis, California 95616   USA

Arthur R. Williams, Ph.D.**
Cornell University
Ithaca, New York 14850   USA

Phoebe D. Williams, Ph.D. *
University of the Philippines
Health Sciences Center
College of Nursing
Quezon City, PHILIPPINES

Martha Stone Wiske, M.A.
20 Temple Street
Boston, Massachusetts 02114   USA

Ruth Wolman, M.A.
Brookline Early Education Project
287 Kent Street
Brookline, Massachusetts 02146   USA

Seiko Yokozawa, R.N., RPN *
School of Public Health Nursing
Aoyama 4-43-7
Morioka-City, Iwata Prefecture
JAPAN

------

*Conference participant
**Conference contributors whose papers
could not be included in this volume
because of space limitations or other
considerations.

Preface

This book contains a selection of papers presented at the September 22–26, 1980 Third International Conference on Early Identification of Children Who Are Developmentally "At Risk." Since 1973, when the participants of the first conference met to discuss the international use of the Denver Developmental Screening Test, there has been a growing acceptance throughout the world of the value of early identification of potential health problems. It is generally, although not universally, accepted that identification, diagnosis, and treatment of a handicapped child early in life does much to improve his or her life status. In many countries of the world, screening for developmental problems and potentially handicapping conditions, such as metabolic disorders that lead to mental retardation if untreated, has become the routine first step of early identification so that necessary treatment can begin at the earliest age possible.

Screening is generally recognized as the application of *quick* and *easily administered* tests to an apparently well population to differentiate between those who have or are at risk of having the condition being screened for from those who do not. Screening is needed to identify that previously undetected child who is in need of further diagnostic and treatment procedures.

The participants in the conference reported here agreed that uniform screening methods across the world are not desirable. Countries such as Denmark, Sweden, and the Netherlands, all with well developed health care systems, can apply procedures much closer to diagnoses than those countries where health care programs are in the early stages of development. Furthermore, the well developed countries have moved from the simple assessment of the child in need of help to the more total ecological assessment of the family, and the childrearing strategies used by parents that influence development.

In addition, those countries in which screening is widespread are finding that special efforts must be made to deal with social class and cultural differences that influence the child's level of response. Marked cultural differences exist in the United States and the Philippines, and to some degree in Japan. For the well developed countries of Northern Europe, the transient labor force from southern and eastern Europe provide some unique health problems.

It became clear at the Third International Conference that many investigators have moved beyond the screening level of early identification to a second level assessment within identified *at risk* populations. This is a desirable effort but not the focus of this book. What the reader will find in this volume is the development, validation, refinement, and utilization of screening scales, as well as substantive discussion of the theory and issues involved in early identification.

Dr. Frankenburg sets the stage in his introduction on the current status and lines of investigation in screening. Following three major child development research workers (McCall, Werner, and Lewis), he discusses the current state of our knowledge of, and methods for facilitating development.

The remainder of the book is devoted to screening efforts and their results. The reader will find that these chapters represent the cutting edge of the work on screening as well as long term systematic efforts. It is hoped that these chapters will assist readers in selecting screening instruments that match their needs or will give them insight into how to refine their own instruments. Through this process, children "at-risk" may receive the treatment they need when it is most likely to have beneficial effects.

N. J. A.

Introduction

William K. Frankenburg

The following chapters are a compilation of presentations made at the Third International Conference on the Early Identification of Children Who Are Developmentally At Risk. The two previous conferences were organized as a forum for presentation of research in developmental screening to promote more research and better research in the field and to facilitate the establishment of collaborative projects. Because a child's development is largely influenced by the child's environment, the conference was designed to include researchers working in a variety of environments in diverse countries of the world.

The first conference in September of 1974 was devoted to research with the Denver Developmental Screening Test (DDST), and the second conference was expanded to include a variety of developmental screening tests. The scope of the third conference, in 1980, was further broadened to address the subjects of both early screening and diagnosis under the more inclusive term of *identification*. To provide a stimulus for discussion and theoretical background, consultants Robert McCall, Emmy Werner, and Michael Lewis were invited to participate as both presenters and discussants. The 1980 attendees agreed that the conference was highly successful in meeting its objectives.

The articles presented in this volume provide a summary of the field of research in developmental screening, where it has come from and where it is likely to be going. The following represent only a few of the points that become apparent in reviewing past activities and future directions in early identification of at-risk children.

One of the common early trends in developmental screening research has been to begin by standardizing a developmental screening test. Standardization establishes a uniformity of procedures for administering a test or scale. In addition, standardization of a scale involves the establishment of norms. The term *norms* implies the word normal, and norms indicate average or normal performance. Thus in standardizations, a representative sample of a population must be secured to ensure that the norms represent the average of the population.

Standardization of the DDST was started in Denver 15 years ago; more recent efforts to standardize the DDST have been undertaken in West Germany, the Netherlands, Chile, Japan, the Philippines, Israel, the People's Republic of China, the French-speaking parts of Canada, and among the Navajo Indians of the United States. The rationale for such efforts has been based on the fact that environmental conditions that influence a child's development vary between countries and generally within a country's subsectors of the population.

Standardizations are designed to yield norms or, more precisely, frequency data of average performance. The purpose of standardization studies is to provide a basis for establishing standards so that the development of a given child can be compared with that of other children within the same population, much as one compares a child's growth measurement to a growth chart. The shortcoming of standardization studies is that the normative data provide information only about central tendencies and the ranges of variables within a specific population. For example, if one were to establish norms on lower socioeconomic families, one would find that dental disease is a common occurrence among 70% of the population, that school failure occurs among 40%, and that hearing problems range from 35% to 78% (Frankenburg and North, 1974; Kaplan et al., 1973). Clearly, norms do not make any real sense in the screening for disease or disorders because norms often fail to differentiate diseased subjects from nondiseased subjects.

The problem is more complex when one looks for potential signs of mental retardation. Norms that have been established on a representative sample of the population are crucial if these norms are to reflect the need for further diagnoses. Thus, in screening for disease, the terms *normal* and *abnormal* are of little utility, whereas the presence or absence of the indicators are useful. For more complex predictions, such as cognitive abilities and their relation to school achievement, norms can serve as guideposts for normal development.

If a limited sample that is not representative of the total population is selected, what often happens—as it did in the Denver studies—is that the persons engaged in such standardization studies fail to see the purpose of developmental screening and, more broadly, the purpose of early identification. The aim of screening as employed most commonly in pediatrics is to facilitate the earlier-than-usual identification and treatment of chronic handicapping conditions to reverse or ameliorate an outcome. Thus, screening and early identification are a secondary form of prevention in that they are designed to alter the outcome once the handicapping process has started. If this purpose of screening is accepted, it then becomes necessary to ask a second question: Do norms identify those who are in need of early treatment? The general experience with use of such norms as they were widely applied a decade ago in automated laboratory screening is that they do not accurately identify subjects who are in need of early treatment. Instead, local norms may be useful in the diagnostic process by making it possible to ascertain the degree to which the deviations may be explained on the basis of local socio-economic and cultural factors.

A second major problem often overlooked by those engaged in early identification of the at-risk child and in developmental screening is that persons who design new instruments fail to start by defining operationally the scope and limits of development or the problem in question. All too often this subject is addressed as an afterthought. For example, one of the reasons the developmental screening portion of Medicaid's Early Periodic Screening, Diagnosis and Treatment (EPSDT) was not implemented as early as other aspects of the program was the lack of concensus on what should be included in the broad category of child development. Some of the various areas that might be considered in that category are emotional, cognitive, social, behavioral, self-help, language, hearing, motor, perceptual, motivational, and temperament characteristics. Because the purpose of early identification of the at-risk child is to facilitate early treatment, new researchers entering the field of early identification need first to define operationally and specifically the handicap they are trying to ameliorate.

In retrospect, this has been a problem with the At Risk Register in Great Britain and in the United States with such federal programs as EPSDT and Child Find. Similarly, the Denver studies and most of those presented in the following chapters have such shortcomings. It is necessary to recognize that even if what the program is trying to predict is something that is operationally defined in quantitative terms, most of the diagnostic measures in child development have limited value. For instance, the studies of Camp et al. (1977) determined that the diagnostic Stanford-Binet was no better than the DDST in predicting school failure 3 to 4 years later.

Naturally, accuracy of prediction requires a preliminary understanding of the pathogenesis of disease and of handicapping conditions. In the broad area of child development, such processes will vary with the particular aspects of child development, whether of temperament, motivation, or language. Although more research needs to be done to better understand these processes, it is important to recognize the inherent limitations in prediction. Early prediction of outcome is highly accurate in the area of genetic screening, but it is far less accurate in the prediction of diseases such as tuberculosis and diabetes, which may arise at any time in the life of the child. As a clearer understanding of these disease processes has been gained, it also has become more apparent that the development of symptomatic disease is governed by a variety of factors, such as age and socioeconomic status. In the area of child development, the processes are far more complex and are governed, perhaps to a greater extent, by the child's environment. The chapters by McCall, Werner, and Lewis deal with aspects of this problem in predicting developmental status. Although each of these authors has a different approach or model, they all generally accept the multifactorial transactional model. Perhaps investigators attempting to predict adult status from infancy data should address themselves to multiple factors and to looking at the rate of a given child's development.

Another issue that needs to be considered is that in establishing the validity of developmental screening and diagnostic procedures, one should attempt to dichotomize the scores into suspect and nonsuspect, diseased or nondiseased. The Denver group was one of the first to apply the concepts of sensitivity (i.e., accuracy in identification of diseased subjects) and specificity (i.e., accuracy in identifying nondiseased subjects). Secondary concepts of predictive values of positives and negatives, co-positivity, co-negativity, and Youden indexes are all further extensions of sensitivity and specificity. In the future, more attention will possibly be given to probabilities rather than to dichotomizing results; it is readily apparent that most screening and diagnostic results vary along a continuum from very normal to very deviant, and the more deviant the early finding, the greater the probability of disease or handicap in later years. This observation holds true whether one is measuring tuberculin reactions, serum phenylalanine levels (to diagnose phenylketonuria), bacterial urine counts (to diagnose bacteriuria), or developmental deviations. For instance, van Doorninck et al. (1978) demonstrated in a recent study that the probability of school failure 5 to 6 years later varied from 89% for those with abnormal DDST results to 63% for those with questionable (borderline) DDST results, and 33% for those with normal results. Illingworth (1963) demonstrated similar findings in predicting later mental retardation from infant diagnostic evaluations.

The availability of such probability data would make it possible for the architects of various community early identification programs to set a cutting point on the basis of local resources and priorities. Just as there are various degrees of deviancy in screening and diagnostic procedures, there are also various intensities or degrees of disease and handicap. For instance, degrees of school failure may be classified along a continuum ranging from institutionalization, special education, special-class placement, repeating a grade, and failing a subject, to being below the class median on achievement test scores. The availability of probability data for several intensities of disease or handicap would also give local program developers the option of selecting the degree of handicap and the cutting point or probability in early identification that is most appropriate for the local conditions. Another reason for the use of various cutting points rather than a single one is that if multiple concurrent screens or diagnostic procedures are used, it is possible to determine the probability of a group of factors in predicting outcome. An application of this approach—presented at the Second International Conference and at the Third Conference—is discussed in Chapter 8. In her study, Coons attempted to determine later school status by examining various combinations of the data from the DDST results that reflect the child's biological integrity and past experiences with environmental ratings of suspect and nonsuspect.

Thus, a child receiving an abnormal DDST score and a suspect home environment score might possibly be at "double jeopardy" for later school failure, while a child receiving a normal DDST score and a nonsuspect environmental score might have minimal probability for later school failure. Other combinations might yield probabilities for school failure that range between these two extremes. In summary, the use of probability data in establishing screening and diagnostic cutting points to separate nonsuspects from suspects will no doubt be employed more commonly as the advantages of such an approach become more widely appreciated.

The final point that must be seriously considered is the ethics of early identification efforts. When professionals mount a public early identification program—whether federally mandated or under the auspices of a private group—the architects of such programs imply that the program will be effective in ameliorating the problem in question. There is a widely held view that the earlier the problem is treated, the better the long-term prognosis will be. Yet this view is not supported for a variety of conditions that may not be treatable, such as color blindness. Early treatment also may not improve the prognosis of childhood diabetes. All too often the proponents of a particular screening program fail to consider that it is unethical to advocate a screening procedure that has not been adequately validated. This is commonly true of developmental screening programs such as those designed to identify emotionally disturbed children. In other cases, treatment may not be available. Also, in many programs, screening, diagnosis, and treatment are insufficiently coordinated, and, as a result, it is impossible to ensure that those who are correctly identified prior to the usual time will actually fare better than if they had been diagnosed at the usual time.

The failure to recognize the limited value of standardization studies, the failure to operationally define what one is seeking to identify, the setting of a single cutting point with the determination of validity in terms of sensitivity and specificity, and the ethical considerations of the early identification of the child at risk, are the four main problems that need to be considered during the next few years if progress is to be made in the early identification of the child at risk. The purpose of this book is to give the reader a perspective of international activities in the field of early identification as well as to present future challenges that must be met if society seeks to promote the development of all children to their full potential.

ACKNOWLEDGMENTS

I wish to express my gratitude to the conference attendees, to Dr. Anastasiow, the primary editor of this book, and to the William T. Grant Foundation for financial support.

REFERENCES

Camp, B. W., et al. 1977. Preschool developmental testing in prediction of school problems. Clin. Ped. 16:257.

Frankenburg, W. K., and North, A. F. 1974. A Guide to Screening EPSDT-Medicaid. U.S. Government Printing Office (SRS) 74-24516.

Kaplan, G. J., Fleshman, J. K., Bender, T. R., Baum, C., Clark, P. S. 1973. Long-term effects of otitis media: A 10 year cohort study of Alaska Eskimo children. Pediatrics 52:577–585.

Illingworth, R. S. 1963. The Development of the Infant and Young Child, 7th Edition. Williams & Wilkins, Baltimore.

van Doorninck, W. J., et al. 1978. Infant and preschool developmental screening and later school performance. In: W. K. Frankenburg, A. W. Fandal, and C. L. Mears (Eds.), Proceedings of the Second International Conference on Developmental Screening. University of Colorado Press, Denver.

To all those who work to
enhance the development of children.

Identifying the Developmentally Delayed Child

Section I

DEVELOPMENTAL MODELS

Chapter 1

The Process of Early Mental Development:

Implications for Prediction and Intervention

Robert B. McCall

This chapter sketches a theoretical conception of early mental development that has implications for the prediction of later mental and developmental status, as well as for the potential effectiveness of remediation and therapy. It focuses on infants with or without risk signs who lack obvious symptoms of identifiable syndromes.

There is good news and bad news. The good news is that many infants who are at risk and/or developmentally depressed in early life can, and do, recover under proper environments and with appropriate therapy. The bad news is that it is, and probably will continue to be, difficult to predict before it is medically obvious which infants will recover from early abnormality and which will not.

A CONCEPTION OF EARLY MENTAL DEVELOPMENT

An Important Distinction

This chapter describes briefly a concept of early mental development that rests on an important distinction, which can be seen in Figure 1 (for complete details, see McCall, 1981). This is a plot according to age of a particular characteristic in perhaps height, weight, or vocabulary. The heavy line is the average performance for a sample of subjects; it represents the developmental function. If the sample on which this plot is based is representative of a species, then the heavy line is the species-

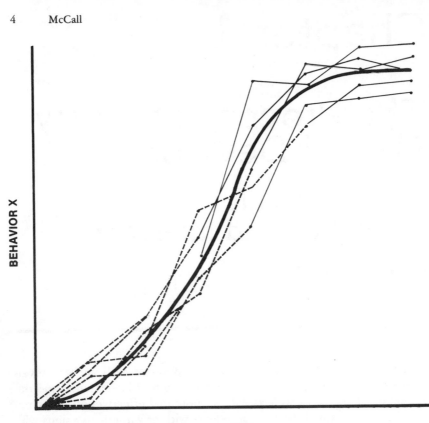

AGE

Figure 1.   A hypothetical plot of the developmental function of a given behavior for five individuals (thin lines) and the developmental function of the group (heavy lines). (Reprinted from McCall et al., 1977, with permission of the Society for Research in Child Development.)

general developmental function—the modal pattern of development for this particular characteristic in the human species.

Developmental functions may be either continuous or discontinuous. They are continuous if the qualitative nature of the trait remains the same across age, as in the case of height, weight, and vocabulary growth. They are discontinuous if the qualitative nature of the characteristic changes from one age to the next, as in the case of Piaget's stages of mental development, which are postulated to change their fundamental nature from stage to stage.

The second characteristic of Figure 1 concerns individual differences, which are represented by the five dashed and thinner solid lines. These might represent plots of five individual subjects, for example. Individual differences are either stable or instable. When they are stable, individuals tend to occupy the same relative rank order in the distribution from age to age. This is reflected in Figure 1 by the fact that the thin lines run approximately parallel to one another near the top of the curve. Individual differences are instable when subjects do not retain their relative rank ordering from age to age, which is depicted by the crossing of the lines at the left of the plot.

The important point, one that is not often appreciated, is that theoretically the nature of the developmental function is independent or unrelated to the stability or instability of individual differences. It is at least theoretically possible for the species to follow a continuous or discontinuous pattern of development and at the same time for individual differences to be either stable or instable. For example, Figure 1 shows a continuous developmental function accompanied by early instability of individual differences followed later by stability. In many respects, the growth of height and general mental performance follows this pattern, with low age-to-age correlations at the beginning that increase to quite high levels during childhood.

Another implication of this distinction is that one set of factors may govern species-general development although quite another set of factors influences individual differences. For example, genetics and maturation may dictate the stages of mentality that all infants pass through from age to age, but temporary environmental factors (adverse perinatal circumstances, infection, etc.) might influence the performance of some babies and not others. That is, grossly exaggerated, biology controls the development of the species, but environment governs individual differences. Again, it is likely that this theme partly characterizes early mental development.

The "Scoop" Conception

Figure 2 is a graphic representation of early mental development referred to as the "scoop"; it portrays a scoop that is slightly elevated at the narrow end. The scoop itself represents the species-general developmental function for early mental development. Developmental time (i.e., age) proceeds from left to right, and the different patterns on the inside of the scoop represent qualitatively different stages of mental abilities. These are the discontinuities in the quality of mental ability from age to age. There are many such stages at the beginning of life and fewer later. Notice also that the scoop is narrow in infancy, indicating that there are few alternative paths or variations within a stage for different individuals to follow. Later in life, the scoop flattens out, rivulets appear in its bottom, and nature allows more qualitative diversity between individuals within a stage.

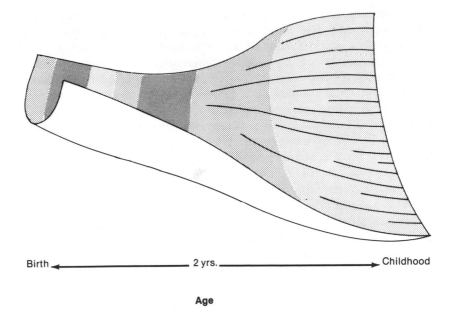

Birth ◄——————————— 2 yrs. ——————————► Childhood

Age

Figure 2.   The "scoop" approach to thinking about mental development. (Reprinted from McCall, 1981, with permission of the Society for Research in Child Development.)

Let ping-pong balls represent individuals. Environmental factors are represented by winds that either blow up and down the scoop, causing the ball to develop faster or slower, or blow across the scoop, altering the qualitative characteristics of the individual within a stage.

Now suppose an individual (a ping-pong ball) begins life at the upper left of the scoop and rolls down toward the right as he or she grows. Notice a few things that can happen on the way to maturity. First, because balls always roll from left to right, they will follow the same set of stages during the course of development, but each stage will be governed in part by qualitatively different factors. Second, in the early months of life, there is a strong self-righting tendency for the ball to return to the main path after an adverse environmental wind, because the sides of the scoop are so steep. This means that temporary deflections caused by perinatal circumstances, infections, even some congenital abnormalities can have an effect on the infant's appearance and performance, but there is a strong tendency for the individual to self-right, get back on the track, recover, and develop toward normalcy. Also, because stages represent qualitatively different skills under the control of partly different sets of factors, infants can "grow out" of some adverse biological and environmental factors more easily than if development were continuous. This is the good news: many infants will spontaneously recover from early developmental delay, and remediation and therapy can have positive effects. If the adverse circumstances are removed early in life, the potential for many children to return to "normal" is substantial.

The bad news of this same principle is that individual differences are not very stable from age to age during this period, because nature, in the form of the steep sides of the scoop, is pushing its wayward children back to a common, fairly narrow, developmental course. The result is that infants who are advanced early in life may or may not be advanced a few months later; and by the same token, infants who are developmentally delayed early in life may or may not be delayed later. Because of this instability of individual differences, predictions made in the early months of life are not very accurate.

Notice that at approximately 2 years of age the scoop flattens out and nature gradually releases its tight grip on the course of development, thus permitting greater variability between individuals. Now the self-righting tendency is less strong, and environmental winds are more likely to have permanent effects. Moreover, the ball is picking up speed, which represents the cumulative effect of experience and the fact that development builds on itself. The result is that individual differences become more stable and consistent from age to age, and they begin to be correlated with environmental and genetic circumstances. Prediction becomes more accurate.

IMPLICATIONS

This conception contains some anomalies. First, species-general mental development and the sequence of stages through which all infants pass are highly governed by genetics, biology, and maturation during the early months of life. At the same time, individual differences are instable and probably the result of temporary environmental and occasionally biological circumstances. Second, despite the popular view that early experience is all-important, it seems that there is greater flexibility and potential for change in early childhood than in infancy. The potential for remediation and environmental intervention to have long-lasting effects is maximal in toddlerhood and early childhood, not in infancy. This is also true because it is at this time that major mental skills—symbolism, verbal fluency, concept formation, logical reasoning—first emerge.

The Good News

The good news is that, of these children who are labeled at-risk or who in the first months of life in fact have delayed development, more turn out to function normally than continue to be delayed or abnormal. For example, in one study involving a portion of the national collaborative perinatal research project sample, three out of every four infants in the lowest 5% of an infant test administered at 8 months had improved beyond the lowest 5% by the time an IQ test was administered between 4 and 9 years of age. They did this either spontaneously or with medical, psychological, and educational help, although for the most part such improvement seemed to occur spontaneously, without professional intervention. Numerous other studies (see Sameroff and Chandler, 1975) show that at-risk infants who are reared in intellectually and emotionally positive environments overcome a variety of initial deficits, and that infants who grow up in extremely deprived or depressed circumstances may remain delayed in developmental performance. Recovery can occur even when the initial depression is caused by biological insult associated with anoxia (Sameroff and Chandler, 1975), although severe biological insults often have persistent effects.

Moreover, a recent study of at-risk infants involving a multidisciplinary team of expert pediatricians, psychologists, social workers, and educators showed that the mental performance outcome in childhood for first-born infants was related more to the socioeconomic status of the parent than to obstetrical or pediatric risk factors, participation in an intervention educational program, or any other factor the investigators measured (Bromwich and Parmelee, 1979; Littman, 1979; Sigman and Parmelee, 1979). Presumably, some aspect of the home environment (or the child's genetic potential) won out over early adversity, a result that supports hope for many depressed infants.

The Bad News

Although most children born at risk or sufferng from early developmental delay recover, all do not. The task is to detect among those at risk who will recover and who will not. Not much progress has been made on this front and for several reasons the task is likely to be difficult.

For one, there are many more infants who are at risk or who actually suffer early developmental delay than there are infants who turn out to have serious problems in childhood and adulthood. For example, much of the knowledge about risk factors comes from retrospective studies of children who have manifested serious developmental delay or other abnormalities. Among such children the rates of severe prematurity, assisted respiration, maternal infection, and other common risk-factors are quite high. But the detection early in life of who will turn out to have a problem requires *pre*diction not *post*diction. Because more children with early risk turn out to be normal than abnormal, the predictive significance of most risk-factors is very small relative to their postdictive significance. Although half the children with syndrome X may have risk-factor Y, only 10% of those infants having risk-factor Y turn out to have syndrome X. This state of affairs can be applied to other areas of human behavior. Almost all heroin users started on marijuana, but only a small percentage of marijuana users become hooked on heroin. Every divorcee got married, but it is not suggested that marriage should be done away with because it leads to divorce. Finally, although there is a tendency among parents who abuse their children to have been abused themselves when they were children, it is not necessarily the case that a substantial proportion of children who are abused will in turn abuse their own children.

Another reason prediction is difficult is that "abnormality" means different things to different individuals, and a single screening test given at a single age is not likely to be able to detect all of the qualitatively different problems that infants and children can develop. Because mental development proceeds in qualitatively different steps or stages, each potentially governed by some common and some unique circumstances, abnormalities and delayed development will appear at different ages/stages depending on the qualitative nature of the abnormality. Severe forms of cerebral palsy might be noticed quite early, but congenital hearing abnormalities might not show up until the middle of the second year. Moreover, each of these three syndromes will affect a different aspect of developmental performance, making it very difficult to detect abnormality with an "omnibus test" at a single age.

Another problem with prediction is that the tendency is to concentrate on those infants who have early risk signs or clearly manifested depressed development from the beginning. As indicated, more of these turn out to be normal than abnormal. The suggestion here is that an infant who begins life normally and shows progressive declines in development is much more likely to have a serious problem than the infant who begins life in a depressed or delayed state. Therefore, testing needs to be done periodically.

A final problem with the prediction strategy is that it has been assumed that once the obviously normal individuals are screened out, prediction is much higher within an at-risk sample than within the general population. Although correlations to later status do appear somewhat earlier and are somewhat higher than those for normal samples, it may come as a shock to many that the correlations are not much higher (Kopp, in press; Kopp and McCall, in press). In fact, if analysis eliminates infants with obvious diagnoses who need no infant test to indicate that they have and will continue to have a problem (e.g., Down syndrome), it is suspected that the correlations will not be usefully higher for at-risk infants than for unselected populations. (See Kopp and McCall, in press.)

CONCLUSIONS

The position taken in this chapter is not totally pessimistic; it is simply held that the prediction task is being addressed in the wrong way. Good clinical pediatric diagnosticians tend to work in the following way. Suppose the patient has symptoms X and Y. These alone may or may not be significant. But if X and Y are accompanied by W, that increases the likelihood that the subject has syndrome A. If X and Y are accompanied by symptoms U and V, the patient may have syndrome B. And if X and Y are accompanied 6 months later by either symptom R, S, or T or some combination of them, then it is likely that the child has syndrome C. But this is not the way screening devices (or most diagnostic instruments) are designed or scored, even though this is the way pediatricians think and use them. Standardized infant tests or screening devices are too general, they lack items salient to make specific diagnoses (e.g., feeding problems, sleep problems, family histories or genetic information, perinatal risk factors, etc.), and no scoring scheme exists for detecting specific syndromes. But screening devices are not "supposed" to do this; it is suggested that in this case they may never be of great predictive value. Rather, it seems preferable to develop assessment tools that imitate the logic of a shrewd pediatric diagnostician that could be given by paraprofessionals. It just has not been done.

But even then, it is too much to expect that it will be possible to detect future abnormalities months or years before they become manifested. Mental development is not continuous, it is not like a balloon being blown up by nature over time, in which everything is present early and simply gets larger wtih development. Rather, mental development is more like the transformations that characterize the growth of butterflies and tadpoles, and although some abnormalities may be manifest at one stage, others may not become apparent until later stages. An infant with congenital deafness may seem quite normal until the parents do suspect something is wrong. Cerebral palsy is so variable in the severity of affliction that some infants with CP may be detectable at birth and others may not be noticed until much later. Therefore, not only do different syndromes appear at different stages, but they become manifest in qualitatively different forms. This makes prediction a much more intricate task than what omnibus infant tests with their limited item pools are capable of accomplishing.

As can be seen, the position here is sympathetic in principle to early and periodic screening and detection for developmental abnormalities and delay, but it is not believed that it is being approached in the best possible way. Later abnormalities must be present in some form in the early months of life and it should be possible to detect them; but success so far has been minimal. Piaget's conception of development as a series of qualitatively distinct stages has not really been taken seriously. It is suggested that the current conception of screening may not be very fruitful, that predictions will increase only when screening and diagnostic tests include items that are known to distinguish between certain syndromes, and that tests are scored in a manner designed specifically to detect different syndromes, as, for example, the Minnesota Multiphasic Personality Inventory is scored.

Nevertheless, the effort is worthy of support. Because the task is more complicated than most researchers thought, it does not follow that it should not be attempted. That attempt, however, should be made not only with renewed vigor but with revised insight.

REFERENCES

Bromwich, R. M., and Parmelee, A. H. 1979. An intervention program for pre-term infants. In: T. M. Field (ed.), Infants Born At Risk: Behavior and Development. Spectrum, New York.

Kopp, C. B. Risk factors in development. In: P. H. Mussen (ed.), Manual of Child Psychology. In press.

Kopp, C. B., and McCall, R. B. Stability and instability in mental performance among normal, at-risk and handicapped infants and children. In: P. B. Baltes and O. G. Brim, Jr. (eds.), Life-Span Development and Behavior, Vol. 4, Academic Press, New York. In press.

Littman, B. 1979. The relationship of medical events to infant development. In: T. M. Field (ed.), Infants Born At Risk: Behavior and Development. Spectrum, New York.

McCall, R. B. 1981. Nature-nurture and the two realms of development: A proposed integration with respect to mental development. Child Dev. Vol. 52, 1, pp. 1–12.

Sameroff, A. J., and Chandler, M. J. 1975. Reproductive risk and the continuum of caretaking casuality. In: F. D. Horowitz (ed.), Review of Child Development Research, Vol. 4. University of Chicago Press, Chicago.

Sigman, M., and Parmelee, A. H., Jr. 1979. Longitudinal evaluation of the preterm infant. In: T. M. Field (ed.), Infants Born At Risk: Behavior and Development. SP Medical and Scientific Books, New York.

Chapter 2

Sources of Support for High-Risk Children

Emmy E. Werner

After decades of concern with pathology, child development research in the mid and late 1970s began to focus on self-righting tendencies in the human organism, which seem to move children toward normal developmental outcomes under all but the most adverse circumstances (Sameroff and Chandler, 1975).

Major forces in this focal swing of the pendulum from illness to wellness have been: renewed interests in evolution and the new field of sociobiology (Freedman, 1979; Wilson, 1978); an outpouring of studies on the competencies of infants (for a review see Osofsky, 1979); and a few longitudinal investigations begun shortly after birth, such as the Coping Project of the Menninger Foundation (Murphy and Moriarty, 1976), the New York Studies of Temperament (Thomas and Chess, 1977), and the Harvard Preschool Project (White, Kaban, and Attanucci, 1979). All have made us aware of the resilience of normal children, that is, their capacity to cope effectively with the internal stresses of their vulnerabilities (such as developmental imbalances) and with external stresses (such as major illnesses, accidents, deaths, or family discord).

Studies of deprived or disadvantaged children in Europe and the U.S., reviewed by Rutter (1979), noted that even with the most distressful homes and the most stressful experiences, some individuals come through unscathed and seem to have a stable, healthy personality development.

Research on the offspring of psychotic parents by Garmezy (1976) at the University of Minnesota and by Anthony (1974) at Washington University in St. Louis has also begun to focus on the "psychological invulnerables," children of mentally-ill parents who display unexpected resilience and creativity.

There is a great need to understand *how* the successful coping patterns of such high-risk children are shaped by situational and personality factors. Protective factors within the children and their caregiving environments that allow them to develop normally in spite of risk, stress, and disadvantage need to be studied more systematically in longitudinal research and incorporated into the design of early identification and intervention programs.

This chapter reviews some of the findings from the Kauai Longitudinal Study (1955–1979) on sources of support within high-risk children and their caregiving environment that contribute to normal psychological development, in spite of chronic poverty and higher-than-average rates of reproductive risk and parental psychopathology. It first examines sex differences in vulnerability and resiliency at birth and in the first and second decades of life. It then identifies coping patterns and sources of support that discriminated high-risk resilient children from peers of the same age, sex, and low SES who developed serious learning and/or behavioral problems in childhood and adolescence. Finally, the study introduces a transactional model of the shifting balance between risk, stress, and protective factors within the child and the child's caregiving environment that seems to account for the range of adaptive and maladaptive outcomes encountered. The implications of the findings are discussed from a cross-cultural perspective, and the importance of informal sources of support in the care of high-risk children are emphasized.

METHODOLOGY

The 698 children whose lives were followed from the prenatal period to young adulthood live on the Island of Kauai, the "Garden Island," at the northwest end of the main islands in the Hawaiian chain. They were born in 1955, when Hawaii was still a territory, and came of age after the islands had become the fiftieth state of the U.S.

The population of this island is a kaleidoscope of different ethnic groups: Japanese, Filipino, part and full Hawaiian, Portuguese, Puerto Rican, Chinese, Korean, and a small group of Anglo-Caucasians. They are for the most part descendants of immigrants from Southeast Asia and Europe who came to Hawaii to work for the sugar and pineapple plantations. About half of the children in this cohort grew up in families in which the fathers were semiskilled or unskilled laborers, and many of the mothers had less than eight grades of formal education.

A detailed account of the methodology of the study is given in two books, *The Children of Kauai* (Werner, Bierman, and French, 1971) and *Kauai's Children Come of Age* (Werner and Smith, 1977). A third book on the resilient children and youth in this study is by Werner and Smith, (1981).

The study began with an assessment of the reproductive histories and the physical and emotional status of the mothers in each trimester of pregnancy, from the fourth week of gestation to delivery. It continued with an evaluation of the cumulative effects of perinatal stress and the quality of the caregiving environment on the physical, cognitive, and social development of their offspring in infancy, childhood, and adolescence.

Independent assessments of the children and their families were made in the perinatal period and in years 1, 2, 10, and 18. The assessments included: evaluations by pediatricians of the severity of prenatal and perinatal complications based on events occurring during the prenatal, labor, delivery, and neonatal periods; home interviews and observations in the prenatal and postpartum periods, and at year 1 by public health nurses; psychologic and pediatric examinations and interviews with the child's caregiver at age 20 months; primary mental abilities and perceptual-motor tests in grade five; teacher's evaluation of classroom behavior, as well as home visits and family interviews by social workers, at age 10; and scholastic aptitude, achievement, and personality tests and in-depth interviews conducted by clinical psychologists with high-risk youth at age 18. In addition, there were diagnostic exams by specialists for children who had "deviant" findings on the developmental examinations given at birth and at ages 2, 10, and 18 years.

Records on file in community agencies for members of the birth cohort and their families were monitored as well. These included social service records, records of family physicians and hospitals, the public and mental health departments, the family court and police, as well as cumulative records in elementary and high schools, the department of special education, and vocational rehabilitation agencies. In addition, through access to the Mental Health Register for the State of Hawaii, referrals for inpatient and outpatient treatment for the youth and their families were monitored.

Thanks to the cooperation of an immensely helpful community, attrition rates throughout the study remained low: 96% of the 1955 birth cohort participated in the 2-year follow-up, 90% in the 10-year follow-up, and 88% in the 18-year follow-up. For a small group ($N = 29$), the offspring of psychotic parents, study data now extends into their 25th year of life (1979).

RESULTS

Approximately one out of every three youngsters in childhood and one out of every five youngsters in adolescence among the youth in the 1955 cohort developed serious behavior or learning problems, some because of major biological insults that prevented adequate development, others because of the poverty of their homes or a persistently disorganized family environment that prevented normal integration. Frequently, several of these risk factors interacted and exposed these children and youth to cumulative stresses that were too difficult to cope with unaided.

Sex Differences in Vulnerability and Resistance to Stress

Sex differences in susceptibility to both biological and psychosocial stress were noted, with boys being found to be more vulnerable in childhood, girls more vulnerable in adolescence.

At birth, more boys than girls in the study had been exposed to moderate or marked perinatal stress ($M = 59$, $F = 51$). More than half (8 of 15) of the boy babies but less than one-fifth (2 of 11) of the girl babies with the most serious perinatal complications died in infancy, most in the neonatal period.

Throughout the first decade of life more boys than girls were exposed to serious accidents or illnesses requiring medical care, and more boys than girls had learning and behavior problems. By age 10, more boys than girls were in need of long-term (6 months) remedial education, or of placement in a learning disability class ($M = 14$, $F = 8$) or class for the mentally retarded ($M = 15$, $F = 10$). In addition, more boys than girls were considered in need of long-term mental health care ($M = 14$, $F = 11$). Contributing factors seemed to be the physical immaturity of the boys, more stringent expectations for male sex-role behavior in childhood, and problems in aggression control. Boys who were at risk because of constitutional factors (moderate-severe perinatal stress; congenital defects; parental, especially maternal, mental illness) were more vulnerable in a disordered caregiving environment than girls with the same predisposing conditions.

Trends were reversed in the second decade of life: the total number of boys with serious coping problems dropped (from 88 to 66) while the number of girls with serious behavior disorders rose (from 54 to 69). More boys than girls were among the proportion of youths with records of serious delinquencies ($M = 77$, $F = 26$), but the sex ratio of other disordered behavior shifted from a majority of boys in childhood to a majority of girls in late adolescence.

Related to this trend was the cumulative number of stressful life events experienced by each sex. Boys with serious coping problems had experienced more adversities than girls in childhood (including birth of younger sib, departure of older sib, parental conflict, maternal mental-health problems, permanent father absence, change of schools). Girls with serious coping problems had experienced more life stresses in adolescence (including maternal mental illness, problems in their relationships with their parents, parental divorce or chronic conflict that led to temporary separation of one parent from the family, and departure of sibs from the household). Of the girls who had serious mental-health problems by age 18, a high proportion became pregnant, married during their teens, and reported marital stress of their own. Financial problems in adolescence were common among both boys and girls with serious coping problems. The overwhelming majority of boys and girls with serious and persistent learning and behavior problems in this cohort were materially poor, but not all poor children developed problems.

Combinations of social, biological, and psychological variables were among the best predictors of serious learning and/or behavior problems in the study. Among these were: a low standard of living at birth and ages 2 and 10; low levels of maternal education (grade eight or less); a low rating of family stability in the first 2 years of life; moderate to severe perinatal stress; moderate to marked physical handicaps at birth and/or age 10; very low or very high ratings of infant activity by the mother at age 1; a Cattell Infant Intelligence Scale DQ below 80 at 20 months; a Primary Mental Ability (PMA) IQ score below 90 at age 10; and need for placement in a learning disability class and/or for mental-health care for a duration of 6 months or more at age 10.

The presence of four or more of these predictors in the records of the children by age 2 seemed to be a realistic dividing line between most children in this cohort who developed serious learning and/or behavior problems (by age 10 or age 18) and most of those who were able to cope successfully with the developmental tasks of childhood and adolescence.

With these data, it became possible to construct a two-way table correlating high risk (four or more predictors) and low risk (three or fewer predictors) with the likelihood of occurrence of later problems among the children and youth in this cohort. Among the 698 children, a majority of 422 (M = 204, F = 218) fell into the low risk/no problem category and followed a normal course of development in the first 2 decades of their lives. A small group, approximately one out of seven (N = 75; M = 38, F = 37) among the low-risk children, later developed learning and/or behavioral problems in response to stressful life events. The picture was reversed among the high-risk children: a majority in this group, two out of three, developed serious learning or behavior problems in the first and/or second decades of life (N = 129; M = 70, F = 59).

Approximately one out of three of the high-risk children, however, did not develop any significant coping problems during the course of the study, despite the presence of four or more risk factors. Among these resilient children there were significantly more girls (N = 42) than boys (N = 30).

Characteristics of Resilient Children Living in Chronic Poverty

These resilient high-risk children were all born and reared in chronic poverty to fathers who were semiskilled or unskilled laborers on the sugar and pineapple plantations of the island. With few exceptions, their standard of living declined during the first decade of their lives as more children were born into the families (number of children in household by age 10: mean for F = 5.40, SD:2.5; mean for M = 4.52, SD:2.00). A second contributing factor was the closing of several of the pineapple canneries that had provided seasonal employment for the mothers. Most mothers had not completed high school, and nearly half had only eight grades or less of formal education (43% of M; 45% of F).

The majority of the resilient high-risk children had been exposed to some reproductive risk, including rates of moderate-severe complications, low birthweight, need for special hospital care in the neonatal period, congenital defects, and moderate to marked physical handicaps that were considerably above the norm for the cohort as a whole, as were rates of early family instability. Yet all 72 children developed into autonomous and competent young adults who "worked well, played well, loved well, and expected well" when they were last interviewed at age 18. None had sought or received any mental health services during the first 2 decades of their lives.

The study contrasted the behavior characteristics and the features of the caregiving environment of these 72 resilient children with high-risk peers of the same age and sex who also lived in chronic poverty, and who developed serious coping problems in childhood and adolescence.

Of the high-risk children who had serious coping problems by age 10, 90 (M = 51, F = 39) needed long-term remedial education (of more than 6 months duration), or special-class placement (LD, MR) and/or long-term mental health care (of more than 6 months duration). All persons, including those in need of mental health care, had serious learning problems in school.

Of the high-risk youth who had coping problems by age 18, 92 (M = 49, F = 43) had a record of serious delinquency or mental health problems necessitating inpatient or outpatient care. The majority (56/92) of these youths had a record of multiple problems, that is, a combination of delinquency and mental health problems, or mental health problems and teenage pregnancy.

A number of constitutional, ecological, and interpersonal variables discriminated over time between high-risk children born and reared in chronic poverty who seemed to be stress-resistant and peers of the same age, sex, and low SES who developed serious coping problems. Many variables that contributed to resilience were common to both sexes, some were unique for each sex.

A higher-than-average proportion of resilient boys and girls were first-borns (43.3% of M; 28.6% of F). Although most had been exposed to some form of reproductive stress, they grew into robust children who had few serious illnesses during the first 2 decades of their lives and recuperated quickly. Their mothers perceived them to be "very active," "cuddly," "affectionate," "good-natured," and "easy to deal with" when they were infants. Independent observers noted their pronounced autonomy and positive social orientation when they were toddlers. Developmental exams in the second year of life showed advanced self-help skills and age-appropriate sensorimotor and language development for most. In middle childhood, these children possessed adequate problem-solving and communication skills, and their perceptual-motor development was age-appropriate. Parent reports and self-reports indicated a balance between instrumental and expressive activities and interests that were not sex-typed.

Characteristics that differentiated between resilient high-risk youth and youth with serious coping problems in adolescence were: a more internal locus of control; a positive self-concept; and higher scores on the California Personality Inventory (CPI) scales for Responsibility, Socialization, Achievement, and Femininity for *both* sexes.

Resilient girls differed from high-risk girls with problems in adolescence on a number of additional personality dimensions, such as Dominance, Capacity for Status, Sociability, Achievement via Independence, Intellectual Efficiency, and Sense of Well-Being.

Key factors in the caregiving environment that seemed to contribute to stress resistance in the midst of chronic poverty were: parental age (younger mothers for resilient males, older fathers for resilient females); the number of children in the family (four or less); the spacing between the index child and next-born sib (more than 2 years); the number and type of alternate caregivers available to the mother within the household (father, grandparents, older siblings); the workload of the mother (including employment outside the household); the amount of attention given to the child by the primary caregiver(s) in infancy; the availability of a sibling as caregiver or confidant in childhood; structure and rules in the household during adolescence; and the presence of an informal multi-generational network of kin and friends, including teachers and ministers, who were supportive and available for counsel in times of crisis.

The families were poor by material standards, but there was a characteristic strong bond between the infant and the primary caregiver during the first year of life. The physical robustness of the resilient children, their activity level, and their social responsiveness were recognized and responded to by the caregivers and elicited a great deal of attention. There was little prolonged separation of the infants from their mothers during the first year of life. The strong attachment that resulted seems to have been a secure base for the development of the advanced self-help skills and autonomy noted among these children in the second year of life.

Though many of the mothers worked for extended periods and were major contributors to family subsistence, the children had support from alternate caregivers, such as grandmothers or older sisters. As older siblings departed from the household, the resilient girls took over responsibility for the care of younger siblings. The employment of the mother and the need for sib caregiving seem to have contributed to the greater autonomy and sense of responsibility of the resilient girls, especially in households where the father was dead or permanently absent. Competence was enhanced by a strong bond between the resilient daughter and the other females in the family—sometimes across three generations (mother, grandmother, older sisters, or aunts).

Resilient boys, besides often being first-born sons, lived in smaller families and did not have to share their parents' attention with many additional children during the first decade of life. There were males in their family who could serve as models for identification (fathers, older brothers, or uncles). There was structure and a code of rules in the household, but less physical crowding. Last but not least, there were peers, friends, and elders who shared similar values and beliefs and whom the resilient youth sought out for counsel and support in times of crisis and major role transitions.

These strong social bonds were absent among the high-risk children who had difficulties coping under stress. The lack of this emotional support was most devastating to children with a constitutional tendency toward withdrawal and passivity, with low activity levels, irregular sleeping and feeding habits, and a genetic background that made them more vulnerable to the influences of an adverse environment.

These youngsters were more often later-born children in large families whose mothers were more frequently pregnant and gave birth to younger sibs before the index child was 20-months-old. They seemed to be less active and socially responsive to their mothers when they were infants and less autonomous to independent observers during the developmental examinations at 20 months. They were sick more often during childhood and they moved and changed schools more often as well. They also lost siblings or close friends through departure or death. They were exposed to more family discord and permanent father absence (which took a greater toll among the boys with serious coping problems) and to maternal mental illness (which took a greater toll among the girls). There were fewer alternate caregivers in the household for these children, even though many of their mothers worked (but more sporadically), and more parental marriages in this group ended in divorce or separation of one parent from the family.

By age 18, most of these youths had an external locus of control orientation and a very low estimate of themselves. They felt that events happened to them as a result of luck, fate, or other factors beyond their control. Professional assistance sought and obtained by community agencies (much more frequently than among the resilient high-risk children) was considered of "little help" to them.

The cumulative number of stressful life events experienced in adolescence differentiated significantly between high-risk youth whose status improved and those whose status deteriorated. Improved youth also had better relationships with their parents during their teens, especially with their fathers, and shared parental attention with fewer children in the household.

Characteristics of Resilient Offspring of Psychotic Parents

Similar child characteristics were found to discriminate between the resilient offspring of psychotic parents (predominantly children of mothers with affective disorders) and offspring of psychotic parents (predominantly children of schizophrenic mothers) who had developed serious problems of their own in adolescence. The study sample is small, hence the results are only suggestive, but they complement the findings from the high-risk children who grew up in chronic poverty.

Of the 1955 birth cohort, 29 children whose parents received treatment for serious psychiatric problems were located (this constitutes about 4% of the total cohort). No claim is made that this is an exhaustive list of all the parents *in need of* mental health care, only that in these 28 families (one with a set of male twins), one or the other parent received mental health care, either on an inpatient or outpatient basis.

There were more boys ($N = 18$) than girls ($N = 11$) among the children whose parents had received treatment for psychiatric problems. Eleven children, including one set of twins (boys) had mothers whose primary diagnosis was depression, eight children had mothers who were diagnosed schizophrenics, five had schizophrenic fathers, and five had depressed fathers.

By the time they reached age 10, 12 of the 29 offspring of these parents (some 40%) had developed serious learning and/or behavior problems; by the time they reached age 18, 16 of the 29 (or 55%) of the youth showed evidence of serious coping problems, such as antisocial behavior or mental health problems. There were twice as many boys as girls. The overwhelming majority had mothers with serious mental health problems, most with a diagnosis of schizophrenia ($p < 0.05$).

Among the resilient offspring of psychotic parents who had *not* developed any coping problems during the first 2 decades of life, the majority (69%) was offspring of depressed parents, mostly mothers with a diagnosis of unipolar or bipolar affective disorders (depression, manic-depressive psychosis).

The resilient children among the offspring of psychotic parents had about the same proportion of moderate-severe perinatal complications as those who developed serious coping problems, a rate double that of the cohort as a whole (24% versus 12%). But they differed from the more vulnerable offspring of psychotic parents in having fewer congenital defects (12% versus 42%; $p < 0.10 > 0.05$).

The resilient offspring of psychotic parents had at least one alternate caregiver in the home (father and mother, older sibling) who seemed to have buffered the chronic stress of parental mental illness, and they had not been separated from their mother during infancy.

The resilient offspring were more often perceived by their mothers as "good-natured" and "easy to deal with" when they were infants, and home observers noted that the mothers' way of coping with their babies during the first year of life was characterized by predominantly positive interactions.

During the 20-months of developmental examinations, the resilient children of psychotic parents were rated high on social orientation, autonomy, and independence. The resilient offspring of parents with serious mental health problems received significantly higher mean-scores on the Cattell Infant Scale of Intelligence and the Vineland Social Maturity Scale, two tests of adaptive and self-help skills, than the offspring who developed learning and/or behavior problems in childhood.

At age 10, more resilient children had higher scores on the Primary Mental Ability factor R, a nonverbal measure of problem-solving skills, and on factor V, a measure of verbal comprehension skills. They showed no impairment on perceptual-motor skills (judging by their performance on the Bender-Gestalt test) and had fewer attentional problems in the classroom and fewer problems with impulse control at school or at home than offspring of psychotic parents who developed serious problems.

In late adolescence, there was a significant difference in locus of control orientation ($p < 0.01$) between the resilient offspring of psychotic parents and youth who had developed serious coping problems. Most resilient youth believed in control of their fate.

A TRANSACTIONAL MODEL OF HUMAN DEVELOPMENT

The results of the Kauai Longitudinal Study seem to lend considerable empirical support to a transactional model of human development that takes into account the bidirectionality of child-caregiver effects.

Figure 1 attempts to show some of the interrelations between major risk-factors at birth, some of the more common stressful life-events in childhood and adolescence that increased vulnerability in the cohort, and protective factors within the child and his or her caregiving environment that increased stress resistance.

It is the shifting balance between risk, stress, and protective factors in the child and his or her caregiving environment, the balance between "undergoing" and "doing" (Wertheim, 1978), that seems to account for the range of adaptive or maladaptive outcomes encountered in the study.

The majority of the children and youth in this birth cohort (some 422 out of 698) were exposed to low risk at birth, led lives that were not unusually stressful, were blessed by a supportive caregiving environment, and coped successfully in childhood and adolescence.

Some 10% of the cohort (M = 30, F = 42), the resilient high-risk children, were exposed to chronic poverty, higher-than-average rates of perinatal stress, and low birthweight and/or parental illness, but they could draw on a number of ameliorative factors in themselves and in their caregiving environment that tilted the balance from "undergoing" to "doing" and led to successful developmental outcomes.

At the other end of the scale were the high-risk children who lived in persistently-disordered family environments that provided little support and who had experienced biological insult, which prevented adequate development (one out of five in the cohort, $N = 129$). The overwhelming majority in this group tended to develop serious and persistent coping problems in childhood and adolescence. A smaller group ($N = 75$) of low-risk children, born in better-off homes to educated mothers exposed to little reproductive risk, also displayed maladaptive behavior in response to serious and chronic life stresses that were not balanced by protective factors within the child and his or her caregiving environment.

To the extent that children were able to elicit predominantly positive responses from their environment, they were found to be stress-resistant, even under conditions of chronic poverty or in a home with a psychotic parent. To the extent that children elicited negative responses from their environment, they were found to be vulnerable even in the absence of biological stress or financial constraints.

Optimal adaptive development thus seems to be characterized by a balance between the power of the person and the power of the social and physical environment. Intervention in behalf of the child can be conceived as an attempt to restore this balance, either by removing risk or stress or by increasing the number of protective factors children can draw upon within themselves or their caregiving environment.

In this study, constitutional factors within the child (temperament, health) seemed to pull their greatest weight in infancy and early child-

(+)Major Risk Factors (at birth)(−)

Chronic poverty
Mother with little education
Moderate-severe perinatal
complications
Developmental delays or
irregularities
Genetic abnormalities
Parental psychopathology

(+)VULNERABILITY(−)

(+)Major Sources of Stress(−)

in Childhood and Adolescence

Birth of younger sib within
two years after child's

Departure or death of
older sib or close friend

Chronic family discord

Parental iilness

Maternal mental illness

Permanent father absence

Loss of job or sporadic
employment of parent(s)

Sib with handicap or
learning or behavior problem

Change of residence

Change of schools

Divorce of parents

Remarriage and entry of
step-parent into household

Foster home placement

Cumulative number of
stressful life events

(For F: teenage pregnancy)

Within the Child

Birthorder

CNS integrity

Few childhood
illnesses

High activity level

Good-natured;
affectionate dis-
position

Responsive to people

Free of distressing
habits (as infant)

Positive social
orientation

Autonomy

Advanced self-help
skills

Age appropriate sen-
sorimotor and per-
ceptual skills

Adequate communi-
cation skills

Ability to focus
attention and control
impulses

Positive self-concept

Special interests and
hobbies

Expressed desire to
improve self

(+)Major Sources of Support (−)
Protective Factors
Within the Caregiving Environment

Parental age

Number and spacing of children

Lack of crowding in household

Additional caregivers besides
mother

Much attention paid to infant
during first year

No prolonged separation from
primary caregiver in first year

Care by siblings and grandparents

Mother has some employment
outside of household

Availability of kin and neighbors
for support

Counsel by minister and teachers

Close friends

Structure and rules in household

Shared values

Access to special services
(health, education, social services)

(+)RANGE OF PROBABLE
DEVELOPMENTAL OUTCOMES(−)
Adaptive   Maladaptive

*N of risk factors
*N of stressful events
*N of protective factors
  in child
  in caregiving environment

Fewer   More
———
More   Fewer

Risk factors
Stressful events
Protective factors
  in child
  in caregiving environment

Figure 1. Model of interrelations between risk, stress, sources of support and coping (based on data from the Kauai Longitudinal Study).* Changes with stage of life cycle, sex of individual, cultural context.

hood, ecological factors (household structure and composition) gained in importance in childhood, as did intrapersonal factors (self-esteem) in adolescence, judging from the weight assigned to these variables in a series of discriminant function analyses.

The contribution of risk factors, stressful life events, and protective factors within the child and his or her caregiving environment changes not only with the stages of the life cycle, but also with the sex of the child and the cultural context in which he or she grows up. In our culture, boys seem to be more at risk at birth and seem to experience more stressful life events in the first decade of life; the reverse is true for girls in the second decade.

Children growing up in traditional societies around the world (and among rural subcultures of our own) may be exposed to higher risks at birth but to fewer stressful events (such as serial divorces) in childhood and may be able to draw on more protective factors in their caregiving environment than children from modernizing and urban industrial societies. In such societies, however, the lives of girls may be constantly more at risk and stressful than those of boys.

Ethnologists and sociobiologists remind us that there are formal species-specific limits to child-caregiver transactions that are adaptive and that the transgression of which spells trouble. Thus, social bonds that evolved during the long history of our species may place certain constraints on both sexes in all cultures, at all times, beyond which a society cannot push its efforts (either by social policy, persuasion, or coercion) to mold the child and his or her caregivers to conform to social demands or ideology.

Societies undergoing rapid social change, whether in the industrialized West or in the modernizing Third World, cannot afford to neglect these social bonds in a single-minded pursuit of technological or economic "progress," or of "environmental control," without risking maladaptive anomalies of development in caregivers and children, inimical to the long-term survival of that society.

IMPLICATIONS

As we watched these children grow from babyhood to adulthood, we could not help but respect the self-righting tendencies within them that produced normal development under all but the most persistently adverse circumstances.

Maybe cooperation with nature's design rather than wholesale intervention and control would be the wisest policy, particularly in the face of present ignorance about the long-term effects of many ambitious social-policies and social programs. Perhaps it is time to give humble recognition to the good possibility that some 3-million years of evolution may have shaped our social behavior and set some constraints.

At present, there is a need to know more about a wide array of what Antonovsky (1979) called "generalized resistance resources," which seems to be as important as sources of strength for the survivors of concentration camps (which he studied in Israel) as for the making of resiliency in children and adolescents.

Among these resistance resources are: adaptability on the biological, psychological, social, and cultural levels; profound ties to concrete immediate others; and formal or informal ties between the individual and his or her community.

More systematic identification of the positive effect of these variables in contributing to "resiliency" and "invulnerability" is needed in addition to more support and a recognition that sometimes social policies and programs may create unintended consequences breaking instead of strengthening social ties that enable humans to hold up under stress.

More systematic examination is needed of the consequences of sib caregiving, which is prevalent around the world and even in this country, once we move beyond the study of small, nuclear middle-class families to those of minority groups. Cross-cultural studies (Werner, 1979) show that child-caregiving seems to be an important antecedent to nurturant and responsible behavior, which leads to strong affective bonds. Although it is presently preponderant in the nonWestern world, child-caregiving may in the future play an important role as an alternative to maternal-caregiving in the West.

The role of grandparents—as sources of support for hundreds of thousands of children in this country who grow up in homes that are poor and broken—must be considered. Some hints were provided in this study and from those of black children in urban mainland ghettos that grandparents can provide continuity and support in an otherwise unstable situation and have a positive "buffering effect" in the midst of family strife and the dissolution of marital ties.

More information is needed about the role of other alternate caregivers in the outside of the home, whether they are uncles, aunts, cousins, neighbors, or members of communal living arrangements. Cross-cultural studies and studies of child abuse have shown that the effect of multiple caregivers on child behavior depends on the ratio of adults to children. Regardless of culture and social-class standing, a mother's emotional stability and warmth toward her children is greater when there are more adults around to help and when she has fewer of her own children around to handle.

Researchers need to examine more closely the implications of studies of family size and birth order and what they can reveal about the contribution of these demographic variables to stress-resistance in children. The Coleman Report (1968) indicated that the best predictor of success in the school system was not whether one was white or black, rich or poor, but whether one was from a smaller as opposed to a larger family. In this study of Oriental and Polynesian children, family size and birth order also seem related to the making of resilience. Families with four children or less were able to provide more attention for the growing boy or girl during the first decade of his or her life than families with more children. More first-born sons in these families held up well under stress, as did more first- and second-born daughters.

Examinations should be made on the effect of parental age, both that of the mother and the father, on their sons and daughters. In this study, the age of the opposite-sex parent (younger mothers for males, older fathers for females) consistently discriminated between resilient children and peers with serious coping problems at ages 10 and 18, even after the effects of birth order were partialled out.

It "made sense" in the past that younger mothers and older fathers might produce children who were biologically less vulnerable and who would grow up in a home where the father was "settled" enough to provide a stable income. Does it "make sense" in the future, at a time when the post-World-War-II babies are making marriages in which the spouses are closer to each other in age than with any other preceding generation in U.S. history, and are having their babies at later ages?

The women in this study are marrying younger men who are psychologically and economically less prepared to deal with their adult lives, while they themselves have reached sexual maturity (age of menarche) earlier than females of previous generations. Yet control of their reproductive processes is now more independently in their hands, thanks to contraceptive pills and liberalized abortion laws.

Do these trends relate to the greater dominance and autonomy noted among the females of this generation? How lasting will these trends be? How will they affect their sons and daughters?

Will these women and their mates provide a different, perhaps more androgynous model of competence and mental health for their offspring than did their parents' generation, a model that includes "being" as well as "doing," nurturance as well as risk-taking for both sons and daughters?

It is surprising to find that so little attention has been paid in child-development research to such a basic demographic phenomenon as age differences between spouses and their social implications.

Outside of the family circle, there is need to explore the impact of other role models. The three most frequently encountered in this study come to mind: the teacher, not just as a provider of skills essential for survival in a technological society, but as a confidant, counselor, and resilient role model; the minister or pastoral counselor; and the "good neighbor."

An informal network of kin and neighbors and the counsel and advice of ministers and teachers were more often sought and more highly valued among the people of Kauai than the services of the mental health professionals. The families of these children preferred personal rather than impersonal bureaucratic relationships in time of stress, as do other minority cultures in the United States and the majority of the people in the nonWestern world.

In many situations, it may make better sense to strengthen available informal ties to kin and neighbors than to introduce additional layers of bureaucracy into the delivery of social services, and it might be less costly as well.

A strengthening of already existing informal support systems could focus especially on those children and families in a community that seem most vulnerable because they—temporarily or permanently—lack some of the essential social bonds that seem to buffer stress: working mothers of young children with no dependable alternatives for child care; single, divorced, or teenage parents with no other adult in the household; hospitalized children in need of special care who are separated from their families for extended periods of time; children of psychotic parents (and the "well" spouse in such a marriage); migrant and refugee children without access to regular schooling or roots in a permanent community.

The central component of effective coping with the multiplicity of inevitable life-stresses seems to be a sense of coherence (Antonovsky, 1979), a feeling of confidence that one's internal and external environment is predictable, and that there is a probability that things will work out as well as can be reasonably expected. The real issue may well be whether the families and societies in which the children grow up and in which they live their daily lives facilitate or impede the development and maintenance of such a sense.

A young child maintains a relatively small number of relationships that give him feedback and shape his or her sense of coherence. It has been shown that even under adverse circumstances change is possible if the older child, or adolescent, encounters new experiences and people who give meaning to one's life and a reason for commitment and caring.

> All living growth is pliant . . .
> and men who stay gentle
> are kin of life.
>
> Lao Tzu (ca 604 B.C.)
> Tao, *The Way of Life*

REFERENCES

Anthony, E. J. 1974. The syndrome of the psychologically invulnerable child. In: E. J. Anthony and C. Koupernik (eds.), The Child in His Family: Children at Psychiatric Risk, pp. 529–544, Vol. III, John Wiley & Sons, New York.

Antonovsky, A. 1979. Health, Stress and Coping: New Perspectives on Mental and Physical Well-Being. Jossey-Bass Publishers, San Francisco.

Coleman, J. S. 1968. Equality of Educational Opportunity. U.S. Office of Education, Washington, D.C.

Freedman, D. G. 1979. Human Sociobiology: A Holistic Approach. The Free Press, New York.

Garmezy, N. 1976. Vulnerable and invulnerable children: Theory, research and intervention. Master lecture on developmental psychology No. 1337, American Psychological Association, Washington, D.C.

Murphy, L., and Moriarty, A. 1976. Vulnerability, Coping and Growth From Infancy to Adolescence. Yale University Press, New Haven.

Osofsky, E. (ed.) 1979. Handbook for Research on Infant Development. John Wiley & Sons, New York.

Rutter, M. 1979. Maternal deprivation, 1972–1978: New findings, new concepts, new approaches. Child Dev. 50:283–305.

Sameroff, A., and Chandler, M. J. 1975. Reproductive risk and the continuum of caretaking casualty. In: F. D. Horowitz (ed.), Review of Child Development Research, pp. 187–244, Vol. IV, University of Chicago Press, Chicago.

Thomas, A., and Chess, S. 1977. Temperament and Development. Brunner/Mazel, New York.

Werner, E. E. 1979. Cross-Cultural Child Development: A View from the Planet Earth. Brooks/Cole Publishing Co., Monterey, Cal.

Werner, E. E., Bierman, J. M., and French, F. E. 1971. The Children of Kauai: A Longitudinal Study from the Prenatal Period to Age Ten. University of Hawaii Press, Honolulu.

Werner, E. E., and Smith, R. S. 1977. Kauai's Children Come of Age. University of Hawaii Press, Honolulu.

Werner, E. E., and Smith, R. S. 1981. Vulnerable, but Invincible: A Longitudinal Study of Resilient Children and Youth. McGraw-Hill, New York.

Wertheim, E. S. 1978. Developmental genesis of human vulnerability: Conceptual re-evaluation. In: E. J. Anthony, C. L. Koupernik, and C. Chiland (eds.), The Child in His Family: Vulnerable Children, pp. 17–36, Vol. IV, John Wiley & Sons, New York.

White, B. L., Kaban, B. T., and Attanucci, J. S. 1979. The Origins of Human Competence. D. C. Heath and Company, Lexington, Mass.

Wilson, E. O. 1978. On Human Nature. Harvard University Press, Cambridge, Mass.

Chapter 3

Developmental Models and Assessment Issues

Michael Lewis
and Jeanne Brooks-Gunn

In the study of exceptional children, the educational and medical perspectives of diagnosis, screening, and intervention have been the favored topics of investigation. In contrast, research with normal children has focused on a description of children's competencies and the changes in their abilities over time (cf., Osofsky, 1979; Meier, 1976; Tjossem, 1976). The techniques and theories used by researchers now studying early development are being applied to the handicapped and at-risk young children (cf., Field, 1979; Kearsley and Sigel, 1979; Lewis and Brooks-Gunn, in press; Lewis and Taft, 1981).

Application of particular developmental approaches to the study of exceptional populations has resulted in some problems. The comments here are addressed to the developmental models and assessment research approaches that are being applied to normal and exceptional infants. Using illustrations from the authors' research on premature and handicapped infants, some of the more successful adaptations of process-oriented techniques used to study normal infants is described. Furthermore, problems in the logic underlying comparative research with normal and exceptional samples and the relative importance of cognitive delay in

This paper was prepared under the aegis of an Early Childhood Research Institute supported by the Bureau of Education for the Handicapped, U.S. Department of Education. The authors wish to thank Aileen Wehren, John Jaskir, and Pamela Ritter for their assistance in data collection and analysis. For further information about the Institute's research, please write the authors, Institute for the Study of Exceptional Children, Educational Testing Service, Princeton, New Jersey 08541.

such comparisons are explored. Finally, the diagnostic categories that have dominated special education and pediatrics are reviewed, the premise being that classification of young exceptional children may be more effective if based on skill assessments rather than on medically and etiologically oriented classification systems.

ADAPTATIONS OF RESEARCH TECHNIQUES

Problems with Current Research

There are numerous problems with much of the current research concerning handicapped infants. First, psychometrically oriented research yields nothing more than a description of the child's general level of functioning—usually represented by a single age-equivalent score or an intelligence quotient. Used in the standard prescribed manner, these measures give no information about the nature of the child's deficit and therefore are of limited use in designing curricula. For example, infant intelligence tests do not predict later cognitive functioning (Lewis, 1976; Meier, 1976) except in cases of severe and profound retardation, cases that are self-evident without giving such tests. Prediction is increased, however, by generating factors at different ages rather than relying on global scores. These factors are considered to represent important age-related capacities. They also address specific rather than global functioning. Recently, factor structures have been generated in normal samples (Lewis and Kreitzberg, 1979; McCall, Hogarty, and Hurlburt, 1972), with certain factors being more likely than others to predict later cognitive functioning. Such an approach would be useful in the study of handicapped infants.

Second, many current techniques focus on developmental milestones; for example, the Alpern Boll Developmental Profile, the Vineland Social Maturity Scale, and the Marshalltown Behavioral Developmental Profile are three commonly used detection instruments that are milestone-based. The major problem is that a child's developmental deficit cannot be picked up until he or she has very definitely missed a major milestone. A further problem with the emphasis on developmental milestones concerns the limited amount of information provided by this type of research. In order for intervention strategies to be successful, it is necessary to identify the specific strengths and weaknesses of the child. The milestones and single-score detection instruments simply do not provide a broad and individualized picture of the child's abilities and deficits. Yet without this picture, it is difficult to determine what type of intervention is needed and what the best approach is for a particular child.

Third, much research concentrates on one or two areas of development to the exclusion of others; specifically cognitive and motor development are emphasized and only minimum attention is given to emotional, social, and communicative development. The selective attention to certain capacities affects the content of intervention programs, because intervention is linked to evaluation of the child's status.

Fourth, the interaction of various capacities has been ignored until recently (cf., Cicchetti and Serafica, 1974). It is clear that the developmental unfolding of skills is not linear but involves the interaction and transformation of a variety of capacities. For example, early cognitive delay affects other areas of the child's functioning, such as interaction patterns and motivational systems. In turn, these affect the child's cognitive ability. As another example, clearly early motoric competencies allow the child to move in space and to reach for objects; activities that lay the foundation (although do not totally account for) the development of cognitive skills such as object permanence (Decarie, 1965).

Fifth, the development of most assessment instruments has not been based on research findings of infant abilities. Not only can the need for research be demonstrated, but in some cases research has in fact been an integral part of instrument development. For example, Lewis, Goldberg, and Campbell (1969) developed a measure of attention and information processing, later using this measure to study attention deficiencies in at-risk populations (Lewis, 1971; Yoshida et al., 1974; Zarin-Ackerman, Lewis, and Driscoll, 1975). The Neonatal Behavioral Assessment Scale (Brazelton, 1973) was developed as a clinical assessment scale refined through the use of normal populations (Sameroff, 1979) and is now being used to assess premature infants (Als, Lester, and Brazelton, 1979).

Current research on handicapped infants is remedying many of these problems. For example, use of single scores that hypothetically reflect the overall functioning of a child is decreasing because single scores do not provide a basis for prediction of later developmental function and do not offer information that is specific enough for use in planning intervention strategies. Research is moving from the use of traditional developmental milestones to the use of techniques that assess the child's functioning within several developmental domains. In addition, the interaction of skills is being emphasized, both within and across developmental domains. Finally, there is growing recognition that research techniques need to be used to gather information about the development of handicapped children (cf., Lewis and Brooks-Gunn, in press; Brooks-Gunn and Lewis, 1980, 1981; Cicchetti and Sroufe, 1976; Emde, Katz, and Thrope, 1978; Simeonsson and Huntington, 1980; Simeonsson, Huntington, and Parse, 1980).

The importance of an intensive and extensive research effort on the development of young handicapped children cannot be overemphasized, especially as it relates to the development of intervention and detection techniques. Research provides the means to study the relationship between age and diagnosis and the interrelationships of skills as a function of both age and diagnostic category. In addition, the focus can be on the development of group categories based on behavioral performance rather than on traditionally used medical categories.

COMPARISON GROUPS AND
THE STUDY OF THE EXCEPTIONAL INFANT

In any study of differences between groups, for example Down's syndrome and normal infants, sick and normal infants, or preterm and term infants, a serious logical problem exists. When testing or assessing group differences, Group A may be statistically different from Group B. The variables and underlying processes that reference this difference are used to indicate how the two groups differ. Thus, for example, preterm and term infants show quite different mother-infant interaction patterns. Mothers of preterm infants are significantly more interactive with their infants than are mothers of term infants (Field, 1979; Divitto and Goldberg, 1979). Preterm-term difference in interactive patterns has been attributed in part to the effects of prematurity. Although the two groups differ, it cannot be logically assumed that the differences are attributable to the specific attributes of the premature group alone. It is now known that term and preterm infants differ on a wide set of variables, not just on prematurity per se (Fox and Lewis, 1981). Preterm infants are not only premature but are often sick; for example, 40% of preterm infants with birthweight of 1,500 grams or less have intercranial hemorrhages (Keller, 1981). In a recent study of preterm healthy infants, preterm sick infants, term healthy, and term sick infants, Lewis and Fox (1980) found that maternal interaction patterns when infants were 3 months of age varied as a function of infant sickness rather than prematurity. Although significant differences were found between preterm sick and term healthy infants (the groups usually compared in the prematurity literature; cf., Field, Dempsey, and Shuman, 1981; Divitto and Goldberg, 1979; Beckwith et al., 1976), term healthy and term sick infants also differed in ways similar to those differences usually reported between preterm and term infants. Additionally, sickness accounted for more variance in maternal interaction patterns than did prematurity. Thus, differences in mother-infant interaction are determined by several variables rather than just one variable. Without several comparison groups, findings may be narrowly interpreted or overdetermined.

Generally, differences between two groups may not be said to be related to a particular cause because the two groups may differ on a wide set of processes and abilities. In order to study the relationships between biological, cognitive, and sociopsychological variables, it is necessary to recognize the error of one-to-one comparisons. Differences between normal children and children with known handicapping conditions may not be attributed to the general attributes of the child unless several groups of handicapped children are tested, with differences occurring between these groups. Thus, if a normal group of infants is compared to a group of Down's syndrome infants, differences between them cannot be attributed to the condition of Down's syndrome unless the differences are shown to be unique to a Down's syndrome-normal infant comparison (i.e., are not seen in a physically impaired-normal comparison where the Down's syndrome and physically impaired children do not differ). Therefore, a third group of children (at the very least) must be studied before any conclusions are made about the effects of a specific (as opposed to general) handicapping condition. Two research examples illustrate the problem of group comparison research. In both, the difference between normal and Down's syndrome infants is not unique to the Down's syndrome children but is found for other handicapped-normal infant comparisons.

Mother-Infant Interaction Patterns

In the first study, children's and mother's interactive patterns were observed (Lewis and Brooks-Gunn, 1980; Brooks-Gunn and Lewis, 1980). Three groups of infants were seen in the first 3 years of life: normal (N = 167), Down's syndrome (N = 61), and physically impaired and developmentally delayed children (N = 59). Mother-infant interaction patterns were observed for 15 minutes of a free play situation. Frequency of specific maternal behaviors and infant behaviors as well as frequency and type of interaction between mother and infant were recorded. Interactions were of particular interest. The interactive measures examined were: 1) amount of maternal initiations, the number of maternal behaviors considered to be initiations of an interaction; 2) amount of maternal responses, the number of maternal behaviors considered to be responses to the infant's initiations; 3) amount of interactions, number of maternal initiations and responses; 4) percent of initiations to total behavior emitted; 5) percent of responses to total behavior; 6) percent of interactions to total behavior; 7) percent of initiations to interactions; and 8) percent of responses to interactions. These measures, rather than reflecting specific maternal and infant behaviors, explore the amount of interaction between mother and child as well as the style of that interaction (i.e., who is initiating and who is responding). This approach and measurement system has been used successfully in research on mother-infant dyads with normal children (Lewis and Lee-Painter, 1974; Lewis, 1972; Lewis and Freedle, 1973; Lewis and Coates, 1980; Lewis and Kreitzberg, 1979). The findings for 1-year-old normal, Down's syndrome and physically impaired infants are presented in Figure 1. (Findings for the 2-year-olds and their mothers were similar to those reported in Figure 1 in terms of differences among groups and, although not relevant to the argument about groups comparisons reported here, age trends from year 1 to year 2 were found; see Lewis and Brooks-Gunn, 1980.)

As can be seen, the Down's syndrome and normal infants differed, but the physically impaired and normal infants also differed from one another. In fact, the response patterns for the Down's syndrome and the physically impaired handicapped group were quite similar. Thus, as argued, a comparison of only Down's syndrome and normal children would have resulted in significant differences that could have been interpreted as a function of Down's syndrome. These differences, however, are not attributable to the Down's syndrome per se—rather, the findings are attributable to differences between normal and handicapped infants. Without a third comparison group, the contribution of the specific etiology of Down's syndrome as separate from the more general condition of being handicapped would not have been assessed.

Visual Self-Recognition

The findings on mother-infant interactions reported here are not unique in that logical problems may exist in any developmental domain. Studying differences between groups and the cause of these differences always requires that more than two groups be compared. Lewis and Brooks-Gunn (1979) have begun to explore the infant's growing sense of self. In order to study this social-cognitive capacity, a test of self-recognition was designed for use with chimpanzees and adopted for use with infants (Gallup, 1970, 1977; Amsterdam, 1972). Children are placed in front of a mirror and their responses to the mirror are observed. After 3 minutes of mirror presentation, a red mark of rouge is applied to the infant's nose. The rouge application is done under the guise of wiping the face so that the child is not aware of the mark (no infants touch the mark immediately after the application suggesting the procedure is successful). Following the application of the mark, infants are placed in front of the mirror again and their self-directed and specific mark-directed behavior is observed. Of particular importance is whether the children use the mirror to direct their fingers to the mark on their noses or to the mark on the mirror image. In several normative samples, no children under 1 year of age touched the mark, and one-fourth of the infants 15 to 18 months of age and three-fourths of infants 21 to 24 months of age recognized the mark. These ontogenetic trends led to study of the ac-

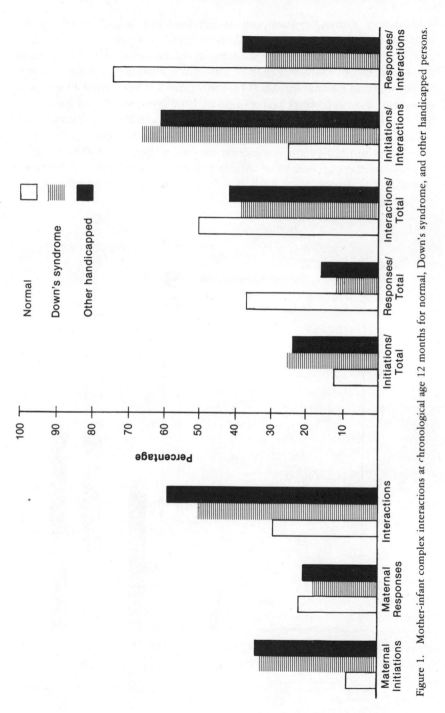

Figure 1. Mother-infant complex interactions at chronological age 12 months for normal, Down's syndrome, and other handicapped persons.

quisition of self-recognition and to development of a theory for early self-knowledge (Lewis and Brooks-Gunn, 1979).

The mark procedure for studying visual recognition has been used by Cicchetti and Sroufe (1978) to look at differences between Down syndrome and normal infants. The procedure has been used to examine the development of mark recognition in three groups—Down syndrome, physically impaired, and normal children (Lewis and Brooks-Gunn, 1980; Brooks-Gunn and Lewis, 1980). These groups are the same as those for which the mother-infant interaction data were presented above. Figure 2 presents the percentage of infants exhibiting mark directed behavior for four age groups (7–12, 15–18, 21–24, and 25–36 months of age)

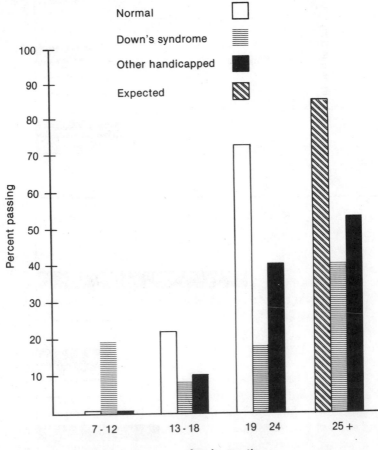

Figure 2.   Mark-directed behavior: normal, Down's syndrome, and other handicapped persons.

for the normal, Down's syndrome, and physically and developmentally delayed groups. First, as can be seen, mark-directed behavior increased over age; second, the two handicapped groups did not exhibit the age-related increases seen for the normal group; and third, the handicapped groups exhibited similar trends. (One Down's syndrome child under 1 year of age touched her marked nose. Because this is the only child under 15 months of age to exhibit mark-directed behavior in over 250 normal or handicapped children seen in this procedure, it is believed to be a random behavior.)

The results of studies of social and cognitive capacity make clear that group comparisons require more than two groups in order to clarify certain logical errors. Studies of normal and Down's syndrome infants claiming that differences are based on Down's syndrome per se are incorrect and misleading. Rather, research, as illustrated by the results presented here, leads to the conclusion that it is the condition of being handicapped rather than a specific condition that affects performance, at least for the measures presented. The task, then, is to explore the processes that mark differences between normal and dysfunctional children and among handicapped groups rather than to apply any particular attribute to a biologically derived label of dysfunction.

COGNITIVE DYSFUNCTION AND DEVELOPMENT

Another issue in the study of young handicapped children has to do with the relative importance of cognitive dysfunction upon skill acquisition. It has been hypothesized, for example, that Down's syndrome children, known to be cognitively delayed, exhibit developmental sequences similar to, although somewhat slower than, normal children. Whether this is true across a wide variety of developmental domains and measures is not known. Continuing with the focus on social and emotional skills, an examination was made of the relationship of cognitive functioning to mother-infant interaction patterns and to infant's responses to mirror image representations.

To examine these relationships, over 53 Down's syndrome infants ranging from 3 to 36 months of age were seen. The infants' responses were examined as a function of chronological age and age equivalents. Age equivalents were determined using the developmental quotient from the Bayley Infant Scales of Development (Brooks-Gunn and Lewis, 1980).

It was anticipated that for some skills, especially those thought to have a central cognitive component, handicapped infants' development would be delayed unless adjusted for developmental age, and that for some skills that are not as closely tied to cognitive development, the use of an adjusted developmental age would not increase the likelihood of approximating normal trends.

Mother-Infant Interaction Patterns

Although it was anticipated that equating the age equivalence would alter normal-handicapped infant differences, age equivalence might not affect all skills equally. Skills involving interactions with other persons might be less influenced than infant competencies. Because others' perceptions of a handicapped infant's skills are based upon both the child's performance (which should be related to age equivalence) and the others' own bias (which may or may not be related to age equivalence), interactions should be less affected by equating children on cognitive ability than on chronological age. Given this hypothesis, it was predicted that mother-infant interaction patterns, which involve not only the child's ability but the mother's perception, would be least affected by equating children for cognitive age equivalence.

In order to look at this effect, mother-infant interaction patterns, as reported in Figure 1, were again observed. Because of the large number of different measures available, only two were focused on: the amount of initiations and responses that mothers exhibit in interaction with their children. These measures include total amount or frequency of maternal interaction and responses (Figure 3), and the ratio of initiations or responses to the total behavior that the mothers exhibited (Figure 4). These data are presented for a sample of 170 normal infants seen at 12 and 24 months of age (Lewis, 1978), for Down's syndrome infants at three chronological ages (3–12, 12–24, and 25–36 months), and for two age groups adjusted for age equivalence through using their Bayley Mental Development Index (MDI) scores (3–12 and 13–24 months).

Maternal initiation increased from year 1 to 2 in the normal sample, but no such pattern was seen for the Down's syndrome group using either age equivalent or chronological age divisions. Maternal responses to infant's behavior increased for both normal and Down's syndrome infants across age with the age equivalence data being the same. The data, then, make clear that equating for age does not change the normal Down's syndrome difference in mothers' initiating behavior. These results strongly suggest that mothers' initiation behavior in free play with their children is affected only partially by their infant's cognitive level, at least as measured by the Bayley MDI.

Self-Recognition

Because self-recognition requires at least some cognitive ability, it was thought that this skill should be affected by age equivalence adjustment (Cicchetti and Sroufe, 1978). The percentages of infants touching their

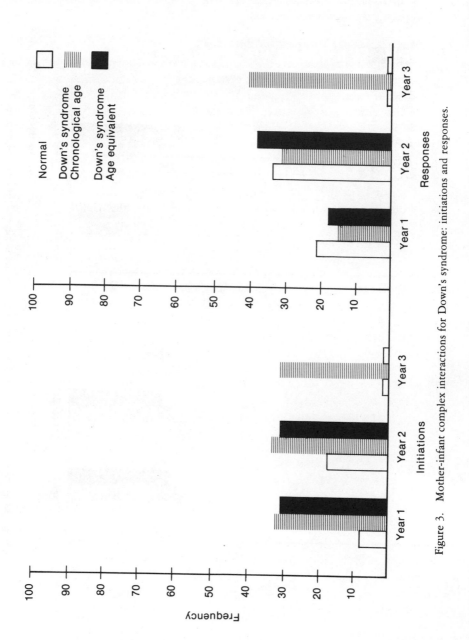

Figure 3.   Mother-infant complex interactions for Down's syndrome: initiations and responses.

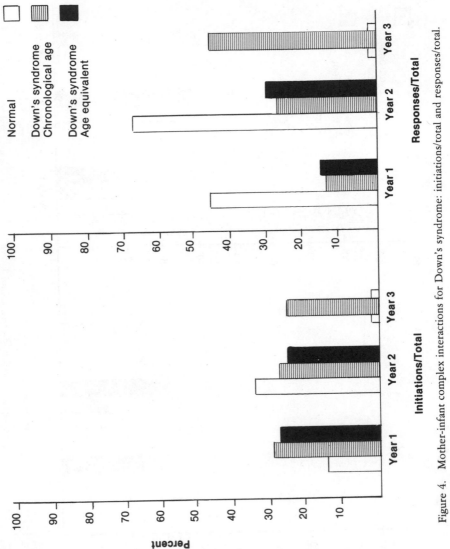

Figure 4.   Mother-infant complex interactions for Down's syndrome: initiations/total and responses/total.

marked noses are presented in Figure 5 for four age groups—7–12, 13–18, 19–24, and 25–36 months of age. Three groups are presented— a normal sample (Lewis and Brooks-Gunn, 1979), Down's syndrome infants by chronological age, and Down's infants by age equivalent using their Bayley MDI scores. As can be seen, no normal infants and one of the Down's syndrome infants recognized the mark at 7–12 months. At 13–18 months, 25% of the normal and 9% of the Down's syndrome infants noticed the mark; and at 19–24 months, these percentages were 67% (normal) and 17% (Down's syndrome). Thus, no significant differences between the normal and handicapped samples appeared until

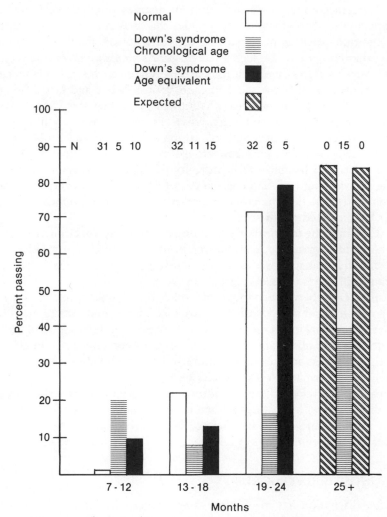

Figure 5. Mirror task: mark-directed behavior.

19–24 months. When age equivalents rather than chronological ages were used, no significant differences between the normal and Down's syndrome infants were found: 13% of the Down's syndrome and 25% of the normal infants touched their noses at 13–18 months, and 80% versus 67% did so at 19–24 months. Thus, age equivalence is more important than chronological age in the expression of mark-directed behavior.

Age Equivalents Other Than IQ

As has been seen, relationships between cognitive and social domains in handicapped infants do exist but are quite complex as specific behaviors tap different competencies and different degrees of cognitive function. Interestingly, some of the competencies that may not be highly related to cognition, such as maternal interactive behavior, may exhibit links with other competencies, such as language. As an example, mother communicative patterns have been shown to be related to the child's language level (Snow, 1972; Snow and Ferguson, 1977). Leifer and Lewis (1978, 1979), comparing the language of mothers of normal and Down's syndrome infants and of the children themselves, found that when the groups were matched on mean length of utterance rather than chronological age, maternal speech to the two groups did not differ, although differences related to language level were found. Thus, mothers seem to be using specific linguistic and context cues rather than child age or overall cognitive dysfunction in determining the pattern of communication with their handicapped children.

Care must be taken when examining cognitive dysfunction as a factor in the child's world, because the relationships may be fairly behavior-specific and domain-specific. Nonetheless, the use of adjustments for certain skill levels (in particular, cognitive and linguistic) seem to lessen the difference between normal and exceptional infants and therefore support the belief that dysfunctions are often associated with retardation of developmental levels rather than the processes underlying these skills. In addition, the observation—of which adjustment, cognitive versus linguistic level, best equates normal and handicapped infants—may be used to provide information on the relationship between skills. Thus, if MDI scores do not alter handicapped/normal differences whereas MLU (mean length utterance) levels do, then we have learned that specific linguistic skills rather than general intelligence is more critical for the behaviors under investigation.

DIAGNOSTIC CATEGORIES

As the discussion has made clear, one process underlying differences between handicapped and normal infants may be the degree of general retardation. Dysfunctions may differ in their levels of developmental delay rather than in process variables. Such a conclusion has been reached by others (Cicchetti, Serafica, and Butterworth, 1980) and the data here seem to support this finding. Thus, rather than Down's syndrome children exhibiting developmental processes different from children with other dysfunctions or from normal children, what may exist is a continuum of developmental delay. Another possibility is that most (but not all) infant competencies are mediated only in part by developmental delay rather than by the handicapping condition. This caveat might be indicated by the few cases where group differences have been demonstrated when dysfunction was controlled (e.g., Dodd, 1975). Regardless of the view taken, it is clear that dysfunction accounts for more variance than do process variables.

These conclusions have implications not only for group differences but for the classification of children and the use of diagnostic labels. The classification system used to distinguish between groups of children is based on a biological/etiological system, a view that is both logical and reasonable within medicine. From a developmental or educational point of view, however, such a classification system is inadequate. If no previous differences between classification groups can be located in a wide set of developmentally and educationally important tasks and skills, the usefulness of the classification system itself may be called into question. It may be the case that these biological/etiological categories are not useful in differentiating children in terms of the general developmental-educational processes that form the bases of intervention programs. Recall that intervention should be predicated on the differential processes and abilities of children. If the current classification system provides us with few between-group differences, then the classification itself may be an inadequate system from an educational point of view.

As an example, Lewis (1981) reported on attentional differences and their usefulness in assessing at-risk infants. This attentional paradigm has been used to distinguish healthy from sick infants (Lewis et al., 1967), Down's syndrome from normals (Hawryluk and Lewis, 1978), and healthy preterms from sick preterms (Lewis, 1981). In a set of studies, differences between birth asphyxia infants and infants suffering from respiratory distress syndrome were compared. It was clear that birth asphyxia and respiratory distress syndrome have different etiologies.

Examination of birth asphyxia and respiratory distress syndrome infants across the first 2 years of life, including tests of attention distribution and language, failed to locate group differences (Lewis, 1981). That is not to say that there are no differences between these two groups of children; it is logically impossible to conclude this. Nonetheless, the lack of apparent differences presents a good example of the point regarding diagnostic classifications. Although classification may be useful for medical intervention, it may be limited in terms of psychological description and educational intervention. Because intervention plans result from assessment of current skills, the lack of group differences suggests that educational strategies should not be based on these classification systems.

Such examples as these raise the possibility that diagnostic categories based on biological/etiological factors, although having value for certain types of intervention, may be highly limited for others. If this is a general observation, the need for an additional classification system becomes clear. Such a classification system must be able to differentiate groups (and individuals) in terms of assessment and along dimensions that are relevant for education intervention strategies in order to be useful for educational intervention. Knowing an IQ score is insufficient for creating an intervention program, just as knowing a child is developmentally delayed or physically impaired is insufficient. A new classification system should be constructed around the educational dimensions amenable to change. It is realized that this is not a simple task; however, the development of a classification system based on a relevant assessment instrument and on educational intervention strategies is a task that requires immediate attention.

SUMMARY

Although considerable progress has been made toward the development and use of detection instruments, too little attention has been given to assessment of children who are at risk or who have a known dysfunction. This chapter addresses three issues relevant to assessment: 1) group comparisons and the need to look across more than two different dysfunctions; 2) the use of age equivalence in understanding developmental processes and group differences; and 3) diagnostic categories and educational intervention. These issues address problems in research, assessment, and classification. The focus on the handicapped child is intended to draw attention to the complexities of known dysfunctions and to demonstrate that classification alone is insufficient from both a process and intervention point of view.

REFERENCES

Als, H., Lester, B., and Brazelton, T. B. 1979. Dynamics of the behavioral organization of the premature infant. In: T. Field (ed.), Infants Born at Risk: Behavior and Development. S. P. Medical and Scientific Books, New York.
Amsterdam, B. K. 1972. Mirror self-image reactions before age two. Dev. Psychol. 5:297–305.

Beckwith, L., Cohen, S. E., Kopp, C. B., Parmlelee, A. H., and March, T. G. 1976. Caregiver-infant interaction and early cognitive development in preterm infants. Child Dev. 46:579–587.

Brazelton, T. B. 1973. Neonatal Behavioral Assessment Scale. Clinic in Developmental Medicine, No. 50. Lippincott, Philadelphia.

Brooks-Gunn, J., and Lewis, M. 1980. The relationship of social and cognitive development in Down's syndrome infants. Paper presented at the International Conference on Infant Studies. April, New Haven, CT.

Brooks-Gunn, J., and Lewis, M. 1981. Assessing young handicapped children: Issues and solutions. Young Except. Chil. 2.

Brooks-Gunn, J., and Lewis, M. Assessing the handicapped young: Issues and solutions. J. of Division of Early Childhood. Vol. 2, 1981, pp. 84–95.

Cicchetti, D., and Serafica, F. 1974. Attachment behaviors of Down's syndrome children in a strange situation. Paper presented at the American Psychological Association Meeting. September, New Orleans, LA.

Cicchetti, D., Serafica, F. C., and Butterworth, G. 1980. An organizational view of development in Down's syndrome infants and toddlers. Paper presented at a Symposium on Social and Cognitive Development in Down's Syndrome Infants at the Infant Study Conference. April, New Haven, CT.

Cicchetti, D., and Sroufe, L. A. 1978. An organizational view of affect: Illustration from the study of Down's syndrome infants. In: M. Lewis and L. Rosenblum (eds.), The Development of Affect: Genesis of Behavior, Vol. 1. Plenum Press, New York.

Cicchetti, D., and Sroufe, L. A. 1976. The relationship between affective and cognitive development in Down's syndrome infants. Child Dev. 47:902–929.

Decarie, T. G. 1965. Intelligence and Affectivity in Early Childhood. International Universities Press, New York.

Divitto, B., and Goldberg, S. 1979. The effects of newborn medical status on early parent-infant interaction. In: T. Field (ed.), Infants Born at Risk: Behavior and Development. S. P. Medical and Scientific Books, New York.

Dodd, B. 1975. Recognition and reproduction of words by Down's syndrome and non-Down's syndrome retarded children. Am. J. Ment. Defic. 80:306–311.

Emde, R., Katz, E. L., and Thrope, J. K. 1978. Emotional expression in infancy: II. Early deviations in Down's syndrome. In: M. Lewis and L. Rosenblum (eds.), The Development of Affect: Genesis of Behavior, Vol. 1. Plenum Press, New York.

Field, T. (ed.), 1979. Infants Born at Risk: Behavior and Development. S. P. Medical and Scientific Books, New York.

Field, T., Dempsey, J., and Shuman, H. 1981. Developmental follow-up of pre- and post-term infants. In: S. Friedman and M. Sigman (eds.), Preterm Birth and Psychological Development. Academic Press, New York.

Fox, N., and Lewis, M. 1981. The role of maturation and experience in preterm infant development. In: J. J. Gallagher (ed.), New Directions in Special Education. Jossey-Bass, San Francisco.

Gallup, G. G., Jr. 1970. Chimpanzees: Self-recognition. Science, 167:86–87.

Gallup, G. G. 1977. Self-recognition in primates: A comparative approach to the bidirectional properties of consciousness. Am. Psychol. 32:329–338.

Hawryluk, M. K., and Lewis, M. 1978. Attentional patterns in infants with Down's syndrome: A preliminary investigation. Paper presented at the Eastern Psychological Association Meeting. April, Washington, D.C.

Kearsley, R. B., and Sigel, I. E. (eds.). 1979. Infants At Risk: Assessment of Cognitive Functioning. Lawrence Erlbaum Associates, Inc., Hillsdale, NJ.

Keller, C. A. 1981. Epidemiological characteristics of preterm births. In: S. Friedman and M. Sigman (eds.), Preterm Birth and Psychological Development. Academic Press, New York.

Leifer, J., and Lewis, M. 1978. Maternal question-asking behavior: A longitudinal analysis. Paper presented at the Eastern Psychological Association Meeting. April, Washington, D.C.

Leifer, J., and Lewis, M. 1979. The maternal response component: Mother's linguistic behaviors following child responses. Paper presented at the Eastern Psychological Association meeting. April, Washington, D.C.

Lewis, M., Bartel, B., Campbell, H., and Goldberg, S. 1967. Individual differences in attention: The relation between infants' condition at birth and attention distribution within the first year. Am. J. Dis. Child. 113:461–465.

Lewis, M., Goldberg, S., and Campbell, H. 1969. A Developmental Study of Information Processing Within the First Three Years of Life: Response Decrement to a Redundant Signal. Monogr. Soc. Res. Child Dev. 34(9) Serial No. 133.

Lewis, M. 1971. Individual differences in the measurement of early cognitive growth. In: J. Hellmuth (ed.), Exceptional Infant (Vol. 2). Brunner/Mazel, New York.

Lewis, M. 1972. State as an infant-environment interaction: An analysis of mother-infant interaction as a function of sex. Merrill-Palmer Q. 18:95–121.

Lewis, M. 1975. The development of attention and perception in the infant and young child. In: W. M. Crickshank and D. P. Hallahan (eds.), Perceptual and Learning Disabilities in Children (Vol. 2). Syracuse University Press, Syracuse.

Lewis, M. 1976. What do we mean when we say infant intelligence scores? A sociopolitical question. In: M. Lewis (ed.), The Origins of Intelligence: Infancy and Early Childhood. Plenum Press, New York.

Lewis, M. 1978. Progress Report to NICHD.

Lewis, M. 1981. Attention as a measure of cognitive integrity. In: M. Lewis and L. Taft (eds.), Developmental Disabilities: Theory, Assessment and Intervention. S. P. Medical and Scientific Books, New York.

Lewis, M., and Brooks-Gunn, J. 1979. Social Cognition and the Acquisition of Self. Plenum Press, New York.

Lewis, M., and Brooks-Gunn, J. 1980. Logical problems in research with exceptional children. Paper presented at the International Conference on Infant Studies. April, New Haven, CT.

Lewis, M., and Brooks-Gunn, J. The Handicapped Infant: New Directions in Research and Intervention. McGraw-Hill, New York. In Press.

Lewis, M., and Coates, D. L. 1980. Mother-infant interactions and cognitive development in twelve-week-old infants. Infant Behav. Dev. 3:95–105.

Lewis, M., and Fox, N. 1980. Predicting cognition development from assessments in infancy. In: B. Camp (ed.), Advances in Behavioral Pediatrics. Jai Press, Greenwich, CT.

Lewis, M., and Freedle, R. 1973. Mother-infant dyad: The Cradle of meaning. In: P. Pliner, L. Krames, and T. Alloway (eds.), Communication and Affect: Language and Thought. Academic Press, New York.

Lewis, M., and Kreitzberg, V. 1979. The effects of birth order and spacing on mother-infant interactions. Dev. Psychol. 15(6):617–625.

Lewis, M., and Lee-Painter, S. 1974. An interactional approach to the mother-infant dyad. In: M. Lewis and L. Rosenblum (eds.), The Effect of the Infant on Its Caregiver: The Origins of Behavior (Vol. 1). John Wiley & Sons, New York.

Lewis, M., and Taft, L. (eds.). 1981. Developmental Disabilities: Theory Assessment and Intervention. S. P. Medical and Scientific Books, New York.

McCall, R. B., Hogarty, P. S., and Hurlburt, N. 1972. Transitions in infant sensorimotor development and the prediction of childhood IQ. Am. Psychol. 27:728–748.

Meier, J. H. 1976. Screening, assessment, and intervention for young children at developmental risk. In: T. D. Tjossem (ed.), Intervention Strategies for High Risk Infants and Young Children. University Park Press, Baltimore.

Osofsky, J. (ed.). 1979. Handbook of Infant Development. John Wiley & Sons, New York.

Sameroff, A. (ed.). 1979. Organization and Stability of Newborn Behavior: A Commentary on the Brazelton Neonatal Assessment. Monogr. Soc. Res. Child Dev.

Simeonsson, R., and Huntington, G. S. 1980. Correlates of developmental progress in handicapped infants and children. Paper presented at a symposium on Social and Cognitive Development in Down's Syndrome Infants at the International Conference on Infant Studies. April, New Haven, CT.

Simeonsson, R., Huntington, G., and Parse, S. A. 1980. Assessment of children with severe handicaps: Multiple problems—multivariate goals. J. Assoc. Severely Handicap. 5(1):55–72.

Snow, C. 1972. Mother's speech to children learning language. Child Dev. 43:549:565.

Snow, C., and Ferguson, C. 1977. Talking to Children. Cambridge University Press, Cambridge.

Tjossem, T. D. 1976. Intervention Strategies with High Risk Infants. University Park Press, Baltimore.

Yoshida, R. K., Lewis, M., Schimpler, S., Ackerman, J. Z., Driscoll, J., Jr., and Koenigsberger, M. R. 1974. The Distribution of Attention Within a Group of Infants "At Risk." Research Bulletin 74-41. Educational Testing Service, Princeton, NJ.

Zarin-Ackerman, J., Lewis, M., and Driscoll, J. 1975. Patterns of visual fixation in the sick, premature: A longitudinal study of the first two years of life. Paper presented at the Society for Research in Child Development meeting. April, Denver.

Section II

SPECIFIC METHODS OF IDENTIFICATION

Chapter 4

Early Identification of Developmentally Delayed Children by Maternal Report:

The Minnesota Child Development Inventories

Harold Ireton

The involvement of parents in the assessment of their young children's development has long been recognized as an integral part of developmental diagnosis (Gesell and Amatruda, 1954). Most clinicians have considerable respect for parents' knowledge of their children's development, especially mothers' knowledge. Systematic methods of obtaining parental information about children's development and data regarding it's validity are not commonly available. Until recently the Vineland Social Maturity Scale (Doll, 1953) has stood virtually alone in this area.

Early identification programs have solicited developmental information from mothers but usually in a traditional "history-taking" fashion, including developmental milestones, often without reference to norms for interpretation. Also, professionals may tend to be suspicious of parental information as "subjective" and to be overly enamored of their own "objectivity." Hence, the most-asked question from professionals planning developmental screening programs is Which test should we use? A more fruitful question is What methods of observation, including parents' reports of daily behavior, professionals' observations, and formal brief tests, might be useful (Ireton, 1977). Also, each method must address the following questions: What does this method add to the data base? What does it contribute to rapport between parent and professional? and What does it contribute to the parents' sensitivity to the child and ability to help the child?

Alternatives for obtaining developmental information from parents include interviews, either informal or structured, such as the Developmental Profile (Boll and Alpern, 1975), questionnaires and inventories, and parent testing of children. The research and clinical experience presented here have been with a maternal report inventory format, beginning with the Minnesota Child Development Inventory. The research has moved from developmental assessment via the Minnesota Child Development Inventory to developmental screening, to developmental review. In the process, concepts have been both broadened and sharpened as more specific issues, including preschool screening and developmental review of infants have been addressed. This chapter describes the evolution of the thinking and research and the child development inventories that have resulted from this research.

MINNESOTA CHILD DEVELOPMENT INVENTORY (MCDI)

The Minnesota Child Development Inventory (Ireton and Thwing, 1974) is a standardized instrument for using mother's observations to measure the development of her child. The Inventory is for the assessment of children 1 to 6 years of age. It is designed to assist in the diagnosis of those children whose development is the subject of concern. The MCDI consists of a booklet and answer sheet for the mother and a profile based upon her responses. The booklet contains 320 statements that describe the developmental behaviors of children in the first 6 years of life. The mother responds YES or NO to each statement to describe her child's present behavior. Scoring is a clerical task involving the use of templates.

The Inventory provides a concise picture of the child's current development according to the mother on a profile of eight scales, including General Development, Gross Motor, Fine Motor, Expressive Language, Comprehension-Conceptual, Situation-Comprehension, Self-Help, and Personal-Social. Results are interpreted in reference to age norms for each sex as developmentally retarded, borderline, or within normal limits. Normative validity of the developmental scales was established by examining the frequency of occurrence of performance significantly below age level for each age group.

The norms of the MCDI profile were established on a sample of 796 white suburban children 6 months to 6½ years of age (395 males and 401 females). The sample was obtained in Bloomington, Minnesota, a suburb of Minneapolis with a population of 80,000. Socioeconomic and family data for the sample indicate that the parents were relatively well educated (fathers' mean, 14.1 years; mothers' mean, 13.1 years). Many of the fathers were occupationally successful (professional-managerial, 43%; domestic, service, labor, 8%). Nearly all families were intact. This population was utilized toward the end of providing reasonable assurance of maternal cooperation and comprehension. This end was realized. The norms should be generalized with caution. The effect of limited maternal education on comprehension and validity remains to be determined.

A subsequent clinical study evaluated the validity of the Minnesota Child Development Inventory by comparing MCDI results with the results of psychological testing (Ireton, Thwing, and Currier, 1977). The subjects were 109 white preschool-age children who had been referred to the Child Psychology Clinic at the University of Minnesota Health Sciences Center for evaluation regarding a variety of developmental problems. Mothers' level of education ranged from 11 to 20 years; 99% of the mothers were at least high school graduates, including 17% who were college graduates. The MCDI was obtained at the time of the psychological evaluation. Inventory results classified as normal, borderline, or developmentally retarded were compared with psychological test results including intelligence, fine motor, and expressive language measures classified in a similar fashion.

Deviations from normal on the MCDI General Development, Fine Motor, Expressive Language, and Comprehension-Conceptual scales are associated with significantly higher rates of deviation on psychological evaluation than the base rates for this clinical population. Retarded MCDI scores are associated with high rates of criterion deviation: 100% for the General Development scale; 91% for the Fine Motor scale; 97% for the Expressive Language scale; and 99% for the MCDI profile as a whole. Deviation on the Comprehension-Conceptual scale is significantly associated with intellectual retardation, but may reflect as well expressive language problems. A Comprehension-Conceptual scale score in the normal range usually contraindicates a diagnosis of intellectual retardation. In most cases where MCDI results and criterion results do not match, one measure or the other is classified in the borderline range.

Ullman and Kausch (1979) utilized the Minnesota Child Development Inventory to describe two populations of children, a Head Start group ($N = 72$) and a nursery school group ($N = 62$), both groups about age 4½ years. The percentage of children whose development was within normal limits, borderline, or delayed was determined for both groups for each scale. Except for the Self-Help scale, the Head Start children showed considerably higher incidences of delay on the developmental scales, for example: General Development, 20% vs. 0%; Expressive Language, 25% vs. 3%; and Comprehension-Conceptual, 17% vs. 0%.

In another study, Colligan (1976) studied the utility of the MCDI in the prediction of kindergarten performance. The Inventory data was obtained at the spring kindergarten roundup. Reading and number achievement at the end of kindergarten were measured by the Wide Range Achievement Test. As a part of this study, Colligan developed the Letter and Number scales from items contained in the MCDI. For 59 children, the MCDI scales correlated with reading achievement (Wide Range Achievement Test) as follows: Letter (0.75), General Development (0.62), Comprehension-Conceptual (0.59), Number (0.51), Fine Motor (0.48), Expressive Language (0.33).

MINNESOTA PRESCHOOL INVENTORY (MPI)

Having developed some confidence in the MCDI and with Colligan's research in mind, the study moved on to the problem of screening for school readiness, specifically kindergarten readiness. At this point, the concept of what needed to be measured was broadened to include adjustment problems and various symptoms, as well as developmental skills. In so doing, an attempt was being made to measure additional factors potentially related to school failure in order to identify those children who were at risk for school failure. The MPI (Ireton and Thwing, 1979) provides for the mother's report of any concerns regarding her child, yields a profile of the child's current development and adjustment, and records certain symptoms of the child.

The Inventory consists of a booklet, an answer sheet, a profile, and scoring templates. The booklet contains 150 statements that describe behaviors of children. The first part of the booklet consists of 87 statements that describe developmental behaviors from 2 to 6 years of age. The second part contains 63 statements that describe adjustment problems and symptoms.

The MPI provides a profile of the child's current functioning on seven Developmental Scales and four Adjustment Scales and detects symptoms in four areas, as shown below:

Developmental scales	*Adjustment scales*	*Symptoms*
Self-help	Immaturity	Motor
Fine motor	Hyperactivity	Language
Expressive language	Behavior problems	Somatic
Comprehension	Emotional problems	Sensory
Memory		
Letter recognition		
Number comprehension		

The scores for the Developmental and the Adjustment scales and the individual symptoms items are recorded on the Minnesota Preschool Inventory Profile.

The profile pictures the child's development and adjustment in comparison to children of his or her age. Percentile norms are based upon a sample of 360 Bloomington, Minnesota, children, 4½ to 5½ years of age, who were assessed in the spring preceding entrance into kindergarten. These norms are primarily for specimen purposes. Users should develop local school norms and cutoff points to provide the most appropriate reference points for interpretation.

Validity of the MPI was studied by comparing Inventory results obtained in the spring preceding kindergarten entry with kindergarten teachers' ratings of overall performance as poor, below average, average, above average, or superior obtained at the end of the school year.

The sample consisted of the 287 Bloomington school children for whom both these data were available. Analysis was in terms of correlation between the two measures and, most important for the identification of individual children who are at risk for school failure, by the congruence between classifications made on the basis of MPI data and classifications made on the basis of teacher ratings. In this analysis, each child was classified as developmentally *delayed* or within age range on each of the Developmental Scales and as *maladjusted* or within normal limits according to the Adjustment Scales. The extreme 5% of the sample was somewhat arbitrarily used to define deviant performance on each scale. Similarly, teacher ratings of kindergarten performance were used to classify each child as *poor* or *adequate*. Teacher ratings yielded 20 children who were identified as *poor* performers in kindergarten. These 20 children became the target individuals the research sought to identify, before the fact, as potentially poor performers in kindergarten.

The correlations between the Developmental and the Adjustment Scales and kindergarten performance are presented in Table 1. The Developmental Scales, except Self-Help, correlate with teachers' ratings of kindergarten performance to a statistically significant degree. The Adjustment Scales do not, except for the Hyperactivity Scale, which shows a statistically significant but low correlation.

Regarding identification of individual children as at risk for kindergarten failures, it is important to remember that in the validation sample of 287 children only 20 (or 7%) were rated as poor performers by their teachers. Perfect identification for the study would be to identify these 20 children as potentially poor performers on the basis of prekindergarten Inventory results, and labeling no children as at risk who subsequently perform adequately.

Table 1.   Correlations between
Developmental and Adjustment Scales
and teachers' ratings of kindergarten
performance

Developmental Scale	Correlation +
Self-help	0.07
Fine motor	0.41***
Expressive language	0.20***
Comprehension	0.44***
Memory	0.51***
Letter recognition	0.56***
Number comprehension	0.24***
Adjustment Scale	
Immaturity	0.07
Hyperactivity	0.12**
Behavior problems	0.04
Emotional problems	0.04

+ Pearson product-moment correlation.
** Significant at 0.01 level.
*** Significant at 0.001 level.

Of 19 children with delays *only* on the Self-Help, Fine Motor, or Expressive Language Scales, none were rated poor in overall kindergarten performance. These scales by themselves are clearly not indicative of poor kindergarten performance.

Of the 21 children with delays on the Comprehension, Memory, Letter Recognition, or Number Comprehension Scales, 12 (or 57%) were rated as poor performers in kindergarten (vs. base rate of 7%; p < 0.01). These scales were successful in identifying 60% of the students (12 of 20) who were rated as poor performers in kindergarten. Using these scales alone, only nine children out of 287 (or 3%) were mislabeled as potentially poor performers.

Data for the Adjustment Scales indicate that 27 of the 28 children who scored in the top 5% on one or more of these scales *but* were within age range on the Developmental Scales performed adequately in kindergarten. In other words, extreme scores on the Adjustment Scales by themselves are not predictive of poor kindergarten performance.

The Symptoms items, together with their frequency of occurrence, are listed at the bottom of the MPI profile. Again, these items by themselves are not indicative of poor school performance. Predictions based on presence of these items could lead to serious errors in overidentification and mislabeling. On the other hand, they need to be taken into account in some fashion. Three of the eight children who were *poor* performers and who were not detected by the Developmental Scales had Symptoms items reported for them: two with both motor and language symptoms, and the third with the uncommon symptom of chronic fatigue.

These data suggest the following in regard to validity and utility: only those Developmental Scales most intimately related to academic performance, namely, Comprehension, Memory, Letter Recognition, and Number Comprehension, are successful in singling out the poorest students. It is likely, however, that the whole array of data gathered by the Minnesota Preschool Inventory—maternal concerns, development in all areas, adjustment, and symptomatology—can contribute to recognizing the child's needs, if these data are judiciously utilized without labeling the child. In other words, the model does seem to be sound.

MINNESOTA PRESCHOOL INVENTORY FORM 3,4 (MPI-3,4)

The Minnesota Preschool Inventory, Form 3,4 has been developed for screening 3- and 4-year-olds. The MPI-3,4 (Ireton and Thwing, 1980a) is similar in format to the MPI but somewhat briefer, consisting of 135 items. the MPI-3,4 is also easier to score. Again, local school norms should be developed to provide the most appropriate reference points for interpretation.

MINNESOTA INFANT DEVELOPMENT INVENTORY (MIDI)

Before describing the Minnesota Infant Development Inventory (Ireton and Thwing, 1980b), it is useful to comment on the concept of developmental review in contrast to the concept of developmental screening. The concept of developmental review emerged from a series of conferences on developmental screening sponsored by the American Association of Psychiatric Services for Children and is described in a report titled "Developmental Review in the EPSDT Program" (Huntington, 1977). Developmental review is intended to provide a profile of the child's abilities and is viewed, potentially, as a facilitation process for most parents and children. Screening focuses on the identification of some children with problems. Developmental review specifies a systematic process for describing the child's current functioning in five areas according to parental report *and* professional observation and for determining the child's developmental status in each area by reference to a developmental map. A detailed description of the developmental review process is beyond the scope of this chapter.

The concept of developmental review as a facilitation process (Stone, 1977) guided the designing of the Minnesota Infant Development Inventory. The MIDI provides a means of reviewing the development of infants in the first 15 months of life. It is as concerned with communication with the mother as with the developmental assessment, and as concerned with enhancing the mother's awareness of her baby's development and her role in that development as with identifying children with developmental problems.

The Minnesota Infant Development Inventory measures infant development in five areas: Gross Motor, Fine Motor, Language, Comprehension, and Personal-Social. It also lets the mother describe her baby and report any problems or concerns about the child. The Inventory consists of a booklet of 75 statements that describe in a sequential fashion developmental behaviors in each area. The items of the Minnesota Infant Development Inventory were derived from earlier research with the Minnesota Child Development Inventory.

The professional may save time when reviewing the infant's development by scanning the mother's report before examining the baby, then simply confirm a few age-relevant items by observation or testing. Or the professional may use the Inventory as a systematic guide for observing the child. Furthermore, the Inventory may be used as an interview guide with the mother. The Minnesota Infant Development Inventory does not yield scores; rather, it provides a picture of the child's activities within a framework for making sound professional judgments. Interpretations about the infant's development are based upon both the parent's report and the professional's observations and examination.

SUMMARY

Involving parents in meaningful ways in the process of developmental review and screening of their young children is a challenging task. The experience derived from the research described here demonstrates that mothers want to be involved in the developmental review process when it is positively construed. The research has evolved from developmental assessment by means of the Minnesota Child Development Inventory, through preschool screening, to the concept of developmental review of infants and children. Developmental review is conceived both as an early identification method for some children *and* as a facilitation process for most mothers and children. As the research evolved, the concepts became broader and sharper and the tasks to be set became clearer and more specific. There is now within reach a systematic framework for developmental review that could inform both parents and professionals, that would be based on parental information and professional observation, and that would utilize both parent report inventories and developmental tests.

REFERENCES

Boll, T., and Alpern, G. D. 1975. The developmental profile: A new instrument to measure child development through interviews. J. Clin. Child Psychol. Spring, p. 25.

Colligan, R. C. 1976. Prediction of kindergarten reading success from preschool report of parents. Psychol. in the Schools, 13:3, 304–308.

Doll, E. 1953. The Measurement of Social Competence: A Manual for the Vineland Social Maturity Scale. Educational Test Bureau, Minneapolis.

Gesell, A. L., and Amatruda, C. S. 1954. Developmental Diagnosis. Hoeber, New York.

Huntington, D. 1977. Developmental Review in the EPSDT Program. U.S. Department of Health, Education and Welfare. The Medicaid Bureau (HCFA) 77-24537, Washington, D.C.

Ireton, H. 1977. Measuring development: Instruments vs. methods of observation. What are the alternatives? Paper presented at the Annual Meeting of the American Association of Psychiatric Services for Children. September, Washington, D.C.

Ireton, H., and Thwing, E. 1974. The Minnesota Child Development Inventory. Behavior Science Systems, Minneapolis.

Ireton, H., and Thwing, E. 1979. The Minnesota Preschool Inventory. Behavior Science Systems, Minneapolis.

Ireton, H., and Thwing, E. 1980a. The Minnesota Preschool Inventory Form 3,4. Behavior Science Systems, Minneapolis.

Ireton, H., and Thwing, E. 1980b. The Minnesota Infant Development Inventory. Behavior Science Systems, Minneapolis.

Ireton, H., Thwing, E., and Currier, S. 1977. Minnesota child development inventory: Identification of children with developmental disorders. J. Pediatr. Psychol. 2(1):18–22.

Stone, N. W. 1977. Approaches to management of the handicapped infant. J. Family Practice, 4:217–221.

Ullman, D., and Kausch, D. 1979. Early identification of developmental strengths and weaknesses in preschool children. Except. Child. September, p. 8–13.

Chapter 5

Neonatal Asphyxia as a Risk Factor:

Early Identification of Developmental and Medical Outcome

Jan L. Culbertson and Peggy C. Ferry

In children at risk for developmental abnormalities, early prediction of developmental outcome is important to plan support services for the family and intervention strategies for the infant. Attempts to detect abnormalities during infancy, or to predict later abilities from the newborn period, have been repeatedly criticized in normal children. Emde (1977) and McCall, Hogarty, and Hurlburt (1972) described transitions in sensorimotor development during infancy that reduce the predictive validity of traditional infant assessment measures. Greater accuracy in prediction of later abilities, however, has been reported in samples of children known to be at risk for neuromotor and developmental abnormalities, particularly when very low scores are obtained on tests of infant development (Ireton, Thwing, and Gravem, 1970).

This chapter focuses on the developmental and medical outcome of infants identified as at risk due to neonatal asphyxia. Specifically, two sets of data are described: 1) longitudinal evaluation data on the 53 asphyxiated infants admitted to the study, with attention to both the type of developmental sequelae and the time at which they can be detected;

This project was funded in part under an agreement with the Tennessee Department of Mental Health and Mental Retardation.

2) preliminary data on a subset of asphyxiated infants with attention to neonatal prediction of later outcome.

OVERVIEW OF TOTAL PROJECT

Subjects

The longitudinal study was conducted on infants with a primary diagnosis of neonatal asphyxia admitted to the Neonatal Intensive Care Unit of Children's Hospital of Vanderbilt University between October 1976 and May 1979. Asphyxia was defined as a 5-minute Apgar score of less than six, or in a few cases by other evidence of severe perinatal asphyxia without confirming Apgar scores (e.g., labor accompanied by signs of acute fetal distress, difficulty establishing initial respirations, or immediate metabolic acidosis). Only infants with an estimated gestation of 37 weeks or greater were included. Infants with sepsis, meningitis, elevated IgM, and/or congenital anomalies were excluded from this study, as were complicated pregnancies, including maternal diabetes, medical illness, and multiple births. Of 92 infants admitted to the Neonatal Intensive Care Unit (NICU) with a primary diagnosis of perinatal asphyxia, 53 were eligible for the study.

Procedure

Follow-up of the asphyxiated infants was conducted at the Comprehensive Developmental Evaluation Center, a multidisciplinary diagnostic clinic in the Pediatrics Department of Children's Hospital, Vanderbilt University. The disciplines of pediatrics, neurology, psychology, speech and language pathology, social work, and special education are represented in the clinic, which provides comprehensive evaluation of infants and young children with developmental and learning problems. The protocol for following asphyxiated infants included evaluation prior to discharge from the NICU and subsequent evaluations at 1-month post discharge, and at chronological ages 3 months, 6 months, 1 year, and yearly thereafter until 8 years of age.

The procedure for follow-up evaluations included obtaining informed consent from the parents and examining the infant prior to discharge from the NICU. Neurological evaluations and social service interviews were conducted at every follow-up visit. Psychological evaluations occurred at 1 month post discharge, at 1 year, and yearly thereafter. Speech and language evaluations occurred yearly beginning at 2 years, with special education evaluation beginning when the infants reached 5 years of age. This report summarizes data from the first 3 years of follow-up and results are based on neurologic, psychologic, and social service evaluations.

Neurologic Evaluation

A complete neurologic examination was performed by a pediatric neurologist. This examination included evaluation of head size, cranial nerves, muscle tone and strength, deep tendon reflexes, cerebellar function, sensation, and age-appropriate special reflexes (i.e., suck, root, Moro, stepping, placing, tonic-neck, grasp). Parents were asked about the presence or absence of seizures, coordination, or visual problems. Neurological findings were reported as normal, clearly abnormal (e.g., cerebral palsy, mental retardation, microcephaly, blindness, and/or deafness), or suspect (e.g., poor head control, slight lag in developmental milestones, hypo- or hypertonia, mild hyperreflexia, or clonus after 4 months of age).

Psychologic Evaluation

Neonatal psychologic measures included the Brazelton Neonatal Behavioral Assessment Scale (Brazelton, 1973), which is discussed in this chapter. Outcome data for the total study were based on yearly psychologic evaluations beginning at 1 year of age. The Bayley Scales of Infant Development (Bayley, 1969) were administered at ages 1 and 2 years. Results were considered normal if both the mental and motor scores fell within one standard deviation of the mean, were considered suspect if one of the scores fell below the average range or if both were between one and two standard deviations below average, and were considered abnormal if both scores were greater than two standard deviations below the mean. At 3 years of age, the McCarthy Scales of Children's Abilities (McCarthy, 1972) were administered. Again, scores falling within one standard deviation of the mean were considered normal, scores falling between one and two standard deviations below were suspect, and scores falling greater than two standard deviations below the mean were abnormal.

Social Service Evaluation

Either one or both parents were interviewed at the time of each follow-up evaluation, using both semistructured interviews and behavioral observation methodology. Attention was directed to the parents' perception of their infant's developmental and medical progress, their feelings of attachment toward the infant, their emotional reaction to the high-risk status of their infant, and their emotional reaction to the information provided regarding the progress of their infant. Factors indicating severe family disruption, including divorce, separation, or other evidence of marital discord, child abuse or neglect, or emotional detachment from their child, were noted.

Results

Through May 1980, the following data are available: 53 infants were eligible for participation in the study and were enrolled in the follow-up program; six (11%) were lost to follow-up prior to 6 months of age; and nine (17%) died prior to discharge from the NICU. Of the 38 children followed longitudinally, 19 (50%) were clearly abnormal at latest follow-up examination (including two who died within the first year of life); eight (21%) were suspect for neurological or developmental abnormalities; and only 11 (29%) were normal in all respects. Thus, 28 of the original 53 infants (56%) were either dead or severely impaired neurologically and cognitively by the end of the first year.

The mean follow-up time was 29.82 months for the 38 children followed longitudinally. Eighty-four percent of the infants were followed at least 1 year, 55% were followed at least 2 years, and 26% were followed for 3 years.

The outcome groups (i.e., normal, suspect, abnormal) did not differ in terms of birthweight, gestation, mode of delivery, Apgar scores, or initial pH.

Social and demographic data were obtained on the families of the survivors followed longitudinally. Categories were assigned to families on the basis of the educational background and employment status of the parents (Stahlman et al., 1973). Ratings of one and two were arbitrarily combined to indicate lower socioeconomic status, and ratings of three or four were combined to indicate higher socioeconomic status. Chi-square analyses revealed no significant differences among the three outcome groups of subjects with regard to socioeconomic status. In the families of normal outcome infants, 64% fell within the lower socioeconomic range, and 80% of the abnormal outcome group fell within the lower socioeconomic range. Approximately 38% of the suspect outcome group fell within the lower socioeconomic range. Other variables such as maternal age at the time of delivery and marital status of the parents were also assessed and revealed no significant differences among groups.

Distribution of disorders in the abnormal group of infants is noted in Table 1. All of the infants classified as abnormal had severe developmental delay, and 17 of the 19 had severe cerebral palsy. Most infants had multiple handicaps, generally severe, with markedly impaired functional capacities (i.e., unable to walk, talk, or feed themselves).

Table 1.   Neurologic and psychologic sequelae
of children followed at least 6 months

Group	Asphyxiated infants (N = 38)	Percent
Normal	11	29
Suspect	8	21
Abnormal	19	50
Cerebral palsy	17	45
Developmental delay	19	50
Seizure disorder	12	32
Microcephaly	9	24
Severe visual impairment	7	18
Hearing loss	1	3
Erb's palsy	1	3

Eight infants (21%) were classified as suspect. Six infants displayed cognitive and/or language delays, with scores falling between one and two standard deviations below average on the Bayley Scales of Infant Development or McCarthy Scales of Children's Ability. Behavior disorders were noted in the remaining two children, and no formal psychological testing was possible because of their lack of cooperation.

The remaining 11 children were classified as normal on the basis of follow-up data for at least 6 months. This group, however, includes two infants who were lost to follow-up after their 6-month evaluation and who may have developed abnormalities at a later time.

Of interest was the time at which developmental and neurological disorders could be detected in these infants defined as high risk because of neonatal asphyxia. Analysis of sequential evaluation data in the three outcome categories (abnormal, normal, and suspect) revealed clear patterns in the time with which disorders could be detected. In the abnormal group, none were normal at the newborn or 1-month post-discharge examination. By 6 months of age, 17 of the 19 were abnormal and the remaining were suspect. By 1 year of age, two had died and all others were clearly abnormal and have continued so. In the normal group, all were either normal or suspect at the 1-month post-discharge examination. By 6 months of age, eight of the 11 normal infants seemed normal, two seemed suspect, and one failed to return for follow-up. By 1 year of age, nine seemed normal and two were lost to follow-up. By 2 years of age, nine were again considered normal and two continued to be lost to follow-up. Of the eight infants considered suspect at their latest follow-up evaluation, six seemed normal at 6 months of age and only two seemed suspect at that time. By 1 year of age, seven seemed normal and only one seemed suspect. By 2 years of age, only one seemed normal, six were suspect, and one was lost to follow-up. Five of the infants received a 3-year evaluation to date and all of these were suspect. ˙

Thus, the majority of infants who were clearly abnormal could be detected by 6 months of age (90% of the cases), and all were detected as clearly abnormal by 1 year of age by standard neurological and/or psychological assessment procedures. Many of the infants in the normal group seemed suspect neurologically at birth, 1-month post-discharge and 3-month exams. By 6 months of age, however, most seemed normal and continued to have normal evaluations after that time. The suspect group had, as expected, a more variable course, with many seeming normal at 6 months of age and even at 1 year of age. Subtle disorders appeared with their increasing ages, however, suggesting that both the suspect and the normal group of infants remain at high risk for developmental or learning problems. Although there was excellent correlation between the findings on neurological examination and psychological assessment with the most severely abnormal children, the study data suggest that more subtle developmental and learning problems are apparent only upon detailed psychological evaluation as the children reach 2 and 3 years of age.

Social service interviews of the families revealed a variety of emotional reactions to the progress of their infant, including denial of handicapping conditions, anxiety, anger directed toward professionals, depression, and/or detachment from their infant. In the group of abnormal infants, there were five instances of severe family disruption, including one mother who abandoned her child to the care of the father and paternal grandmother, and a father who abandoned his family within 2 years of the child's birth. In the family of an infant who subsequently died, there was severe marital discord and the family considered institutionalization of the infant prior to her death. In a fourth family, there was concern about extreme maternal detachment from her infant. In a fifth family, both parents experienced prolonged denial (greater than 3 years) of their infant's handicap. The infants in each of these families were severely handicapped with multiple disorders of cerebral palsy, mental retardation, microcephaly, and suspected visual impairment. Although reactions of other parents of abnormal infants were not as extreme, many reported instances of disruption in the family routine due to the demands of caring for their handicapped child.

Instances of family disruption occurred to a lesser degree in families of normal and suspect infants. In two families of suspect children, and one family with a normal child, parents cited difficulty managing their child's behavior. There was concern about one mother of a normal child, an unmarried teenager, who seemed detached from her infant. Anxiety was prevalent in the families of normal and suspect children even after 1 or 2 years of follow-up due to their fear that future developmental problems would be detected in their children.

NEONATAL MEASURES AS PREDICTORS OF OUTCOME

Preliminary data from a subgroup of 12 infants who received more extensive neonatal measures, including the Brazelton Neonatal Behavioral Assessment Scale (BNBAS) (Brazelton, 1973) and the Neonatal Perception Inventory (NPI) (Broussard and Sturgeon, 1970), are presented below.

Subjects

The subjects were 12 of the original group of 38 asphyxiated infants, who were followed longitudinally. They were born between November 1977, and May 1979. Eleven of the 12 had been followed at least 1 year (one of 12 died at 1 year of age), and eight of the 11 survivors were followed for 2 years. Six fell in the abnormal outcome category and six were normal at latest follow-up.

Procedure

The BNBAS was administered at the 1-month post-discharge visit. The results were analyzed according to four a priori clusters of behaviors in the neonate (Adamson et al, 1975): 1) interactive processes (including alertness, cuddliness, and orientation to visual and auditory stimulation); 2) motoric processes (including tone, activity, reflexes, and maturity of movement); 3) organization of state (including degree of irritability, lability of states, and ability to be consoled); and 4) physiological response to stress (including frequency and timing of startles, tremors, and color changes). Results were classified as normal if each cluster score was average or above average. Results were classified as suspect if one or two cluster scores were abnormal and results were classified as abnormal if three or four cluster scores were abnormal.

In addition to the BNBAS, the Neonatal Perception Inventory (NPI) was administered to all mothers at the 1-month post-discharge visit. The NPI was developed to examine the mother's early perceptions of her infant's physical appearance, behaviors, and temperament within the context of her own preconceived expectations and hopes of what her infant should be like. The mother was asked to compare her infant with her concept of the average infant on six behavioral items: crying, spitting, feeding, elimination, sleeping, and predictability. The scores were examined to determine if mothers rated their infants as *better than, less than,* or *the same as* the average infant. Broussard and Sturgeon (1970) have shown that in cases where primiparous mothers rate their 1-month-old infants as less than or equal to the average infant, there is far greater likelihood that the infant will have emotional or developmental problems at 4–5 years of age. Thus the NPI has been shown to have predictive value for infants at high risk for later developmental problems. In the study discussed here, the NPI was administered to mothers regardless of their parity in an attempt to examine their earliest impressions of their infant's behavior. It was hypothesized that infants who were eventually abnormal at 1 year of age would be more likely to be judged as less than average by their mothers at 1 month of age.

Results

The validity was determined of the BNBAS administered at 1 month post discharge in predicting outcome at 1–2 years of age. The BNBAS was quite successful in predicting extremes of developmental outcome. All infants who received a normal Brazelton rating at 1 month were subsequently normal at 1 year, and all those with an abnormal Brazelton rating at 1 month were subsequently abnormal at 1 year. A suspect rating on the Brazelton, however, was not predictive of outcome. Of four suspect ratings, two were later normal and two were abnormal ($X^2 = 7.82$; df $= p < 0.02$). Although the sample was much too small to draw definite conclusions, the preliminary data support the need for continued research with the BNBAS with children identified as at risk for neuromotor or developmental problems.

A further comparison of the 1-month neurological examination results with the BNBAS revealed agreement on five of six infants with an abnormal outcome. On the discrepant case, the BNBAS correctly predicted outcome. The BNBAS and neurological examination results were in agreement on only three of the six normal infants, with the neurological examination correctly predicting two of the three discrepant cases.

The Neonatal Perception Inventory results were less encouraging than the BNBAS results with regard to predicting outcome of the infants. Of the four infants considered high risk for future developmental problems based on their mother's rating, three were eventually abnormal and one was normal. Of the seven infants considered low risk, five were eventually normal and two were abnormal. The results were not statistically significant ($X^2 = 5.41$; df $= 1$; N.S.). Attempts to use the mother's perception of her infant's behavior as a predictor were possibly confounded by such factors as a difference in parity among mothers or briefness of the period of follow-up. Broussard and Sturgeon (1970) have suggested that in addition to measuring the effects of the infant's behavior on the mother, the NPI may be indicative of the mother's feelings of confidence about her mothering skills or her confidence as an individual. Additional information about the mother's attitude toward her pregnancy, the nurturing she received as a child, and her own preparation for becoming a mother would be helpful in understanding her responses to the NPI.

DISCUSSION

Longitudinal outcome data on a group of infants who suffered neonatal asphyxia and who were considered at risk for developmental and medical sequelae are presented here. The data reveal that using standard neurological and psychological evaluation procedures, early detection of severe abnormalities was possible in the majority of cases (90%) by 6 months of age, and in 100% of cases by 1 year of age. Infants who eventually were suspect had a variable developmental course and were difficult to diagnose at an early age. Infants who were normal at outcome often seemed suspect at an earlier age. Because more subtle abnormalities have emerged in the suspect group with increasing age, the normal group should be considered at continued risk for subtle abnormalities that may occur at later ages.

The incidence of death and severe sequelae in the study population exceeded that of other studies involving follow-up of asphyxiated infants. Scott (1976) reported that 17 of 23 (74%) of the survivors in his study, which included both term and preterm asphyxiated infants, had no apparent intellectual or neurological sequelae at 3½–7 years of age. When only term infants were considered, nine of 14 (65%) were normal and five of 14 (35%) had cerebral palsy.

In the Collaborative Perinatal Project (Niswander, Gordon, and Drage, 1975), both term and preterm asphyxiated infants were compared with a control group on intelligence and motor tests at 4 years of age. No significant differences were found between the two groups, leading the authors to conclude that asphyxia is not a major cause of neurological sequelae in the surviving child.

Both Neligan, Prudham, and Steiner (1974) and Brown et al. (1974) reported lower incidence of sequelae than what was found in our study. The difficulties in defining asphyxia (e.g., lower Apgar scores, meconium staining, abnormal fetal monitoring) and the variance in gestational age between infants in this study and those in other studies may partially explain the discrepancy. The study data suggest, however, that in the group of infants termed *asphyxiated infants,* there is a high incidence of brain damage. Furthermore, the emotional and financial toll on families who must care for these severely handicapped children is apparent, with several instances of extreme family disruption occurring in the study population. The impact of these neurologically handicapped children on their families supports the need for early detection of sequelae, early intervention to provide support for the families, and most of all, prevention.

REFERENCES

Adamson, L., Als, H., Tronick, E., and Brazelton, T. B. 1975. A Priori Profiles for the Brazelton Neonatal Assessment. London: Spastic International Medical Publication, 1973.

Bayley, N. 1969. Bayley Scales of Infant Development. Psychological Corporation, New York.

Brazelton, T. B. 1973. Neonatal Behavioral Assessment Scale. Lippincott, Philadelphia.

Broussard, E. R., and Sturgeon, M. S. 1970. Maternal perception of the neonate as related to development. Child Psychiat. Hum. Dev. 1:16–25.

Brown, J. K., Purvis, R. J., Forfar, J. O., and Cockburn, F. 1974. Neurological aspects of perinatal asphyxia. Dev. Med. Child Neurol. 16:567–580.

Emde, R. N. 1977. Two developmental shifts in infant biobehavioral organization: Two Months and Seven-Nine Months. Paper presented at the Biennial Meeting of the Society for Research in Child Development, March, New Orleans, LA.

Ireton, H., Thwing, E., and Gravem, H. 1970. Infant mental development and neurological status, family socioeconomic status and intelligence at age four. Child Dev. 41:937–946.

McCall, R. B., Hogarty, P. S., and Hurlburt, N. 1972. Transitions in infant sensorimotor development and the prediction of childhood IQ. Am Psychol. 27:728–748.

McCarthy, D. 1972. Manual for the McCarthy Scales of Children's Abilities. Psychological Corporation, New York.

Neligan, D. M., Prudham, D., and Steiner, H. 1974. The survivors of clinical asphyxia. In: D. M. Neligan (ed.), The Formative Years. Oxford University Press, New York.

Niswander, K. R., Gordon, M., and Drage, J. J. 1975. The effect of intrauterine hypoxia on the child surviving to 4 years. Am. J. Obstet. Gynecol. 121:892–897.

Scott, H. 1976. Outcome of severe birth asphyxia. Arch. Dis. Child. 51:712–716.

Stahlman, M. T., Hedvall, G., Dolanski, E., Faxelius, G., Burko, H., and Kirk, V. 1973. A six-year follow-up of clinical hyaline membrane disease. Pediat. Clin. North Am. 20:433–446.

Chapter 6

A Comparison of Strategies for Identifying Children in Need of Mental Health Services

Craig Edelbrock

The early identification of emotional and behavioral disorders among children and youth is a fundamental prerequisite to the prevention of psychopathology. Early identification is particularly important in the case of children because behavioral disorders must be viewed with respect to their overwhelming implications for future development, as well as to their impact upon current functioning. Detection of the precursors of child psychopathology would permit early intervention, and in theory at least, the amelioration of such disorders before they produce severe or chronic disabilities.

Despite this rationale for early identification, screening for psychopathological disorders has proved to be less practicable than screening for problems in other areas. Whereas acceptable procedures are available for identifying a wide range of childhood disabilities (such as anemia, tuberculosis, vision deficits, and hearing loss), it has been more difficult to recommend acceptable procedures for detecting emotional and behavioral disorders (Frankenburg and Camp, 1975).

Why? There are no simple answers to this question. The hindrances to effective screening of emotional and behavioral disorders in children are pervasive and complex. Consider, for example, that child psychopathology is not a single well-defined disorder, but encompasses any number of behavioral deviations, emotional states, and patterns of maladjustment, which interfere with normal functioning and developmental progress. Despite efforts to achieve consensus regarding the diagnosis of child psychopathology (e.g., American Psychiatric Association, 1980) there is little agreement regarding the existence, symptomatology, causes, and appropriate treatments of such disorders. It is also difficult to conceive of such disorders as residing "in the child," in that children rarely refer themselves for mental health services or report on their own behavioral and emotional difficulties. Thus, the assessment of child psychopathology depends upon the judgments of adults—usually parents, teachers, or mental health workers—regarding the adequacy of the child's behavioral functioning. Such judgments are far from being perfectly reliable or valid.

There are additional obstacles to screening for emotional and behavioral disorders of childhood. Effective screening depends in part on determining both the prevalence of a disorder in the target population and prognosis in the absence of early intervention. It is also essential to establish that early intervention is more effective than later intervention (or no intervention at all). Unfortunately, few epidemiological studies have been done on adequate samples of children (c.f., Graham, 1979), and prevalence rates depend largely on how the disorders are defined and measured. Likewise, there have been few longitudinal follow-ups of children manifesting specific disorders and few controlled treatment studies. Thus, both the prognosis of childhood disorders and the efficacy of treatments have yet to be determined.

Given these limitations, one can seriously question whether screening for emotional and behavioral disorders can or should be undertaken. Nevertheless, the rationale for the early identification of emotional and behavioral disorders is clear, and such disorders are within the federal screening mandate. Moreover, some evidence suggests that a large proportion of disturbed children do not receive appropriate services. As one clinician put it, "Referral for mental health services is largely an accident. For every child we see there are many others with equally serious problems who do not receive professional help." Thus, the general conviction among mental health professionals is that children referred for services represent only the "tip of the iceberg" in that the majority of disturbed children are unserved.

Given our state of ignorance regarding child psychopathology, it is premature to screen children for specific disorders. At the same time, it is necessary to identify children in need of mental health services, despite the fact that it is difficult to specify the disorders that such children manifest or which treatments are most appropriate. How can we begin to identify such children? A preliminary step involves the development of assessment materials and procedures that tap the behavioral and emotional problems of disturbed children. More accurate description of disturbed children, however, does not solve all problems related to early identification. The complex problems of diagnosis and treatment formulation must still be tackled by clinicians who render mental health services. Nevertheless, more precise assessment of child psychopathology will help lay the foundation for determining who needs services, why services are warranted, and which services are most appropriate.

PROGRESS IN ASSESSMENT

Considerable progress has been made in recent years regarding the assessment and classification of children's behavioral disorders (see Achenbach and Edelbrock, 1978; O'Leary and Johnson, 1979, for reviews). Several instruments meet standards of reliability and validity, and although they have some shortcomings, they are useful as screening devices. Rutter (1967), for example, has developed a 26-item screening inventory for completion by teachers. Adequate test-retest, and interrater reliability has been demonstrated, and despite the crude level of data obtained, the scale discriminates significantly between normal and clinically-referred children.

Behar and Stringfield (1974) expanded Rutter's questionnaire by adding ten items judged to be appropriate for preschool-age children. Factor analysis of teacher ratings for the 36-item Preschool Behavior Questionnaire (PBQ) produced three factors labelled Hostile-Aggressive, Anxious-Fearful, and Hyperactive-Distractible. Significant differences between normal and deviant groups have been obtained for all three scales, as well as for the total PBQ score.

An 11-item screening inventory for the identification of early school maladaption has been developed as part of the Primary Mental Health Project (Cowen et al., 1973). Of the 11 items, five tap Aggressive-Outgoing behavior, five measure Moody-Internalized behavior, and one reflects Learning Disability. Two-week test-retest reliabilities for primary-school teachers' ratings ranged from 0.80 to 0.86 for the three subscales and total score. Moreover, scores have been shown to differentiate significantly between children referred for school mental health services and nonreferred children.

Langner and his coworkers developed a 35-item screening inventory for detecting psychiatric impairments in children ages 6 to 18 years (Langner et al., 1976). The total score has been found to correlate significantly with psychiatrists' ratings of impairment and referral for mental health services. Finally, Kohn and Rosman (1972a, 1972b, 1973) developed Social Competence and Symptom Checklists that produce two bipolar factors labeled Interest-Participation vs. Apathy-Withdrawal and Cooperation-Compliance vs. Anger-Defiance. The reliability and stability of teachers' ratings obtained with these instruments have been thoroughly documented, and sources on both dimensions have been shown to distinguish efficiently between normal and disturbed samples (Kohn and Rosman, 1973).

Although useful in many ways, these instruments have several shortcomings that limit their application as general screening devices. First, three of these instruments (Behar and Stringfield, 1974; Kohn and Rosman, 1973; Rutter, 1967) have been developed and standardized on a narrow age range. Second, these instruments cover only a small set of behavioral symptoms, which restricts the nature of disorders that can be detected. In general, screening instruments produce a single maladjustment score or scores reflecting maladjustment in two global areas, variously labelled Antisocial vs. Neurotic (Rutter, 1967), Hostile-Aggressive vs. Anxious-Fearful (Behar and Stringfield, 1974), Aggressive-Outgoing vs. Moody-Internalized (Cowen et al., 1973), and Anger-Defiance vs. Apathy-Withdrawal (Kohn and Rosman, 1972a, 1972b, 1973). Reliance upon such global behavioral dichotomies may preclude the detection of children manifesting behavioral symptoms related to specific syndromes, such as depression or hyperactivity.

Third, most screening instruments have been developed on combined samples of boys and girls, despite the fact that boys and girls differ markedly in the prevalence and patterning of behavioral problems. Rutter (1967), in validating his 26-item questionnaire, used the same cutting score for boys and girls. Thus, for validation purposes, children with scores of nine or more were considered "disturbed," and those with scores of less than nine were considered "normal." On the average, however, boys in the sample had higher scores than girls. The use of the same cutting score for all children resulted in more false-negative errors for girls (32.5%) than boys (22.1%) and more false-positive errors for boys (9.7%) than girls (4.6%). It is likely that the use of separate cutting scores for boys and girls would have substantially improved screening efficiency.

Finally, problems in establishing validity have plagued all efforts to develop procedures for detecting emotional and behavioral disorders. It is much more difficult to establish morbidity criteria for psychopathology than for medical diseases. Langner et al. (1976) had three criteria against which to validate their 35-item screening inventory: 1) psychiatrists' ratings of impairment based on 654 parent-reported child characteristics, 2) direct psychiatric assessment based on a 1½ hour interview with the child and a ½ hour interview with the child's mother, and 3) actual referral for mental health services. Although any of these indices may be used as a morbidity criterion for child psychopathology, correlations among the three criteria were remarkably low: $r = 0.29$ between referral and direct psychiatric assessment, $r = 0.37$ between total impairment rating and direct assessment, and $r = 0.51$ between total impairment rating and referral. Obviously, the apparent efficiency of a screening procedure will depend upon which criterion is selected for validation purposes.

Achenback and Edelbrock (1981) argued that actual referral for mental health services is the most appropriate criterion against which to validate screening procedures. Direct psychiatric assessment is of limited value as a criterion because it has the weakest relations with other criteria and suffers from low interrater reliability ($r = 0.50$). Referral for services, on the other hand, typically signals persistent problems on the part of the child that have been detected by parents, teachers, or other adults through their observations and interactions with the child in natural settings over an extended period of time. Referral for services is admittedly not a perfect criterion for psychopathology, because false-positives can result from parental oversensitivity to normal child behavior, and false-negatives can result from parental insensitivity to pathognomonic behavior and pressure from others to seek help. Referral may also be related to such factors as availability of services, race, and socioeconomic status.

Whereas referral for services is not a perfect morbidity criterion, it may be the most acceptable of those currently available. It is important to note, however, that significant group differences do not ensure that a screening instrument can discriminate efficiently between referred and nonreferred children. For the screening inventory developed by Cowen et al. (1973), significant differences between referred and nonreferred were obtained for all scales, but scale means and standard deviations (Cowen et al., 1973, p. 30) indicate that the distributions of scores for the two criterion groups overlapped considerably. Hence, it is likely that even the use of optimal cutting scores would result in a substantial proportion of false-negative and false-positive assignments. Thus, significant differences between criterion groups do not necessarily translate into the efficient screening of individuals.

THE CHILD BEHAVIOR CHECKLIST AND PROFILE

The purpose of this chapter is to explore the use of the Child Behavior Checklist and Profile as a means of identifying children in need of mental health services, and in the process, to compare various screening strategies. Although the Checklist and Profile were not developed as screening instruments per se, they can serve this purpose because they depend upon parent ratings of their child's behavior rather than on judgments of trained professionals, and are not difficult or time-consuming to administer or score. In addition, the Checklist and Profile may overcome many of the shortcomings of previous screening instruments and offer a more refined basis for the detection and diagnosis of child psychology. Specific advantages of the Checklist and Profile include: 1) appropriateness for children ages 4 to 16, 2) coverage of a wide range of behavioral problems and adaptive competencies, 3) ability to screen for global maladjustment as well as for behavioral deviations confined to particular syndromes, 4) separate development and standardization for boys and girls, and 5) usefulness in both the detection and diagnosis of child psychopathology.

The Child Behavior Checklist is comprised of 118 behavior problems and 20 social-competence items designed to be reported by parents or parent surrogates. The Checklist is self-administered and requires approximately 15 to 17 minutes to complete. Parents respond to the behavioral-problem items on a 0-1-2 scale: 0 indicates that the item is *not true* of the child, 1 indicates that the item is *somewhat or sometimes true*, and 2 indicates that the item is *very or often true*.

The Child Behavior Profile includes three a priori social-competence scales designed to reflect school performance, involvement in activities, and social relationships. It also includes behavior-problem scales that have been derived separately for each edition through factor analyses of Checklists filled out by parents of children referred for mental health services. To reflect age and sex differences in the prevalence and patterning of behaviors, separate editions of the Profile are being developed and standardized for each sex at ages 4 to 5, 6 to 11, and 12 to 16. Nine reliable behavior-problem factors were obtained for boys ages 6 to 11 and 12 to 16, and for girls ages 6 to 11, whereas eight reliable factors were obtained for girls ages 12 to 16 and boys ages 4 to 5 (Achenbach, 1978; Achenbach and Edelbrock, 1979). The Profile for girls ages 4 to 5 has not yet been completed.

Second-order factor analyses have shown that the first-order, narrow-band behavior-problem scales for each edition form two broad-band groupings that have been labelled Internalizing and Externalizing. The narrow-band factors obtained for each age and sex group and their relations to the broad-band Internalizing and Externalizing factors have been summarized elsewhere (Achenback, 1978; Achenbach and Edelbrock, 1979). Norms have been constructed for the scales of each edition of the Profile by computing normalized T-scores from Checklists filled out by 1,300 randomly selected parents of normal children.

In clinical facilities, the Checklist serves as a guide to the clinical interview with the parents and as a problem-oriented record listing the presenting symptoms reported by the parent. Information obtained from the Checklist is scorable in terms of the Profile, which portrays reported problems in a standardized format and permits comparisons with normal children of the appropriate age and sex. Because it provides quantitative measures of reported behavior, the Profile is also useful in assessing changes in reported behavior over time and in response to treatments. In addition, cluster analysis has been used to identify groups of disturbed children manifesting similar patterns of problems (Edelbrock and Achenback, 1980). These taxonomies are useful in research regarding the etiology, epidemiology, prognosis, and treatment of child psychopathology.

The Validation Sample

Actual referral for services was used as the criterion against which to validate the screening strategies. Comparison of random samples of referred and nonreferred children, however, would introduce possible biases, because of inherent differences in racial distributions and socioeconomic status (SES). Moreover, a random sample of referred children would be overrepresented by certain groups, such as boys ages 6 to 11, who dominate mental health referrals. A validation sample was constructed, therefore, consisting of 50 referred and 50 nonreferred children of each sex at each age from 6 to 16, yielding a total sample of 2,600. Within each age and sex group, referred and nonreferred children were matched on race and SES, so as to approximate an 80:20 ratio of whites to blacks and a normal distribution of SES as indexed by Hollingshead's (1957) seven-step scale for breadwinner's occupation.

Data on the referred sample were obtained from parents whose children had been referred to one of 30 East Coast mental health facilities, which included community mental health centers, child guidance clinics, private· practices, and health maintenance organizations. The Hollingshead scale averaged 3.7 (SD = 1.7) for the referred sample. Data on the nonreferred sample were obtained by interviews with parents in randomly selected households in Washington, D.C., northern Virginia, and southern Maryland. Children qualified for the nonreferred sample if they had not been referred for mental health services in the previous year. The sampling procedure and method of data collection for the nonreferred sample have been described in detail by Achenbach and Edelbrock (1981). The nonreferred sample averaged 3.7 on the Hollingshead scale (SD = 1.64).

The Data

The data consisted of a Child Behavior Checklist completed for each child. For the referred sample, respondents consisted of 83% mothers, 11.5% fathers, and 5.5% others (e.g., foster parents, grandparents). The respondents for the nonreferred sample were 83.1% mothers, 13.5% fathers, and 3.4% others. Several types of information can be derived from the Checklist. First, parents' responses to the individual behavior-problem and social competence items can be analyzed. Second, Profile scores can be computed for the empirically derived behavior-problem syndromes and for the three a priori social-comptence scales labelled Activities, Social, and School. Third, global indices of maladjustment can be obtained by calculating the total behavior-problem score, which is the sum of the parents' responses to all 118 behavior-problem items. A global index of social competence can be obtained by summing the scores on the three social-competence scales (although the School scale is not scored for 4- and 5-year olds). Extensive reliability and stability analyses for these data have been reported elsewhere (Achenbach, 1978; Achenbach and Edelbrock, 1979, 1981). Overall, test-retest and inter-rater reliabilities for the Checklist and Profile data have been high. One week test-retest reliabilities have ranged from 0.72 to 0.99 for Checklist and Profile scores for nonreferred children (Achenbach, 1978; Achenbach and Edelbrock, 1979).

Screening Strategies

Previous analyses have indicated that scores on almost all Checklist items distinguish significantly ($p < 0.01$) between referred and nonreferred children (Achenbach and Edelbrock, 1981). Furthermore, highly significant differences ($p < 0.001$) between referred and nonreferred children have been obtained for all behavioral-problem and social-competence scales, as well as for total behavior-problem and social-competence scores. As described previously, however, significant differences between criterion groups do not necessarily translate into efficient screening procedures. Several strategies were compared, therefore, on their ability to correctly classify normal and referred children. The strategies involved the use of: 1) total behavior-problem score, 2) combined total-behavior-problem and total-social-competence scores, 3) scores on the empirically-derived behavior-problem scales and three social-competence scales that comprise the editions of the Profile, and 4) discrimination analyses applied to the individual Checklist items. To account for age and sex differences in behavior, all four strategies were evaluated separately for boys and girls ages 4 to 5, 6 to 11, and 12 to 16.

Total Behavior-Problem Score

The most global index of psychopathology that can be derived from the Checklist is total behavior-problem score. This index has a distinct advantage in mass screening in that it requires only a few seconds to score from a completed Checklist. Previous analyses have revealed that total behavior-problem score yields the largest separation between normal and referred samples. Summing across all age and sex groups, clinical status accounts for 44% of the variance in total behavior-problem score (Achenbach and Edelbrock, 1981). Nevertheless, the distributions of total behavior-problem scores for referred and nonreferred children still overlap. In determining screening efficiency, therefore, it is necessary to select a cutting score above which children are considered to be positive cases (that is, they resemble children who have been referred for services) and below which children are considered to be negative cases (that is, they resemble children who have not been referred for services).

Selection of optimal cutting scores in an a posteriori fashion would result in artificially high screening efficiency. Thus, it is desirable to select a cutting score based on an independent estimate of the prevalence of psychopathology in the general population of children. Epidemiological studies have indicated that the incidence of psychopathological disorders among children range between 5% and 20% (see Graham, 1979, for review). For purposes of this study, a conservative estimate of 10% was chosen. The total behavior-problem scores corresponding to the 90th percentile for normal children were thus used as the cutting scores. Children with scores above the 90th percentile were considered to be positive cases, whereas those with total behavior-problem scores at or below the 90th percentile were considered to be negative cases. Separate cutting scores were used for boys and girls of the three different age ranges.

Combined Behavior-Problem and Social Competence Scores

The second screening strategy involved determining whether the additional use of the total social-competence score improved upon the screening efficiency of the total behavior-problem score alone. Whereas the presence of behavioral problems may be more likely to precipitate referral for services than the absence of social competence, it seemed likely that screening efficiency could be increased through the use of dual criteria that reflected both problem behaviors and a lack of adaptive competencies. As in the case of the total behavioral-problem score, a base rate of 10% was assumed for selecting cutting scores for the total social-competence scale. It is the absence, however, rather than the presence of social competencies that indicates psychopathology. Thus, cutting scores corresponding to the 10th percentile for total social-competence scores were selected, and children with scores less than the 10th percentile were considered to be positive cases. Children with total social-competence scores at or above the 10th percentile were considered to be negative cases. In using the dual criteria, a child was considered to be a negative case only if he or she fell within the normal range on both scales. In other words, positive cases were determined by positive assignments on either or both of the scales. Cutting scores for the total behavioral-problem and social-competence scales for each age and sex group are shown in Table 1.

Syndrome Scores   As discussed previously, the disadvantage of using global maladjustment scores, such as total behavioral-problem score, is that they are not sensitive to behavioral deviations confined to specific behavioral syndromes. A proportion of false-negative assignments, for example, may consist of children manifesting behavioral symptoms associated with a single syndrome. Such children manifest deviant behavior with respect to one syndrome but do not obtain high global maladjustment scores. Hence, screening strategies involving the use of syndrome scores derived from the Child Behavior Profile were evaluated. For each age and sex group, children's scores on each of the behavior-problem and social-comptetence scales were calculated.

For the behavior-problem scales, the 98th percentile was selected as the cutting score for determining positive cases. Conversely, the 2nd percentile was selected for the social-competence scales. Thus, only 1% to 2% of the normal children would exceed the cutting scores on any scale. Because there are from eight to nine behavior-problem scales and two to three social-competence scales for the various editions of the Profile, this would yield a baseline rate of 10% to 24% if all scales were

Table 1.   Cutoff points for total behavior-problem and social-competence scores[a]

Group	Total behavior problem score	Total social competence score
Boys		
4–5	42	9.0[b]
6–11	40	15.5
12–16	38	15.5
Girls		
4–5	42	9.5[b]
6–11	37	16.0
12–16	37	16.0

[a] For total behavior-problem score, cutoff scores represent the 90th percentile for nonreferred children of each age and sex group, with the exception of the 88th percentile for girls ages 4–5. For total social-competence score, cutoff points represent the 10th percentile for each group, rounded to the nearest 0.5.

[b] For 4- to 5-year-olds, the total social competence scores does not include the School scale.

independent of one another. Two strategies were compared. First, in order to be considered a positive case, a child had to exceed the 98th percentile on at least one behavior-problem scale. Second, the criterion of scoring less than the 2nd percentile on at least one social-competence scale was added.

Discriminant Analysis   A common strategy for distinguishing between criterion groups is the use of linear discriminant analysis. According to this statistical procedure, a weighted combination of items is constructed that best discriminates between criterion groups. Because the optimal selection and weighting of items tends to capitalize to some degree on chance variations, however, it is necessary to test the discriminant functions on independent cross-validation samples. For each age and sex group, therefore, stepwise discriminant analysis was applied to the behavior-problem and social-competence items for a random half-sample of subjects. The stepwise addition of items to the discriminant functions was stopped when no items could contribute signiicantly (p < 0.01) to the predictive equation. The discriminant functions were then evaluated on their ability to classify the subjects in the remaining random half-samples.

RESULTS

The screening procedure based on total behavioral-problem score resulted in a total false-problem rate of 9.4% and a total false-negative rate of 25.4%. This yields an overall error rate of 17.4% In other words, this screening strategy resulted in approximately 82.6% screening efficiency. It should be noted that the efficiency of screening procedures must be compared to the efficiency of using population base rates alone (Meehl and Rosen, 1955). For the specially constructed validation sample, predictions based on base rates would result in an overall error rate of 50%, because this sample consists of equal proportions of referred and nonreferred children. The combined total behavior-problem and social-competence scores resulted in slightly more false-positives (15.4%) but substantially fewer false-negatives (15.7%). This resulted in an overall misclassification rate of 15.5%. The screening procedure based on behavior-problem syndromes produced an overall error rate of 18.2%, comprised of 14.8% false-positives and 21.6% false negatives. The addition of social-competence scales to this screening strategy resulted in only a slight decrease in the overall error rate to 17.6%, but produced almost equal false-positive and false-negative error rates. Very few behavioral-problem items (range three to seven) contributed significantly to the discriminant functions obtained for the various age and sex groups. Application of these discriminant functions to the cross-validation samples resulted in 17.4% misclassifications overall (10.9% false-positives and 23.9% false-negatives).

DISCUSSION

The results indicate that the Child Behavior Checklist and Profile are useful in screening children in need of mental health services. Given the imperfect criterion of referral for services, approximately 82% to 84% of the children in the validation sample could be correctly assigned according to clinical status. Several options are available for using the Checklist and Profile for screening. For screening large groups of children, the total behavior-problem score provides a quick and easy procedure for detecting global maladjustment. The use of the combined total behavior-problem and social-competence scores increased the proportion of false-positives slightly, but resulted in the best overall screening efficiency. If false-positives are considered to be more costly than false-negatives, a higher cutting score, such as one corresponding to the 95th or 99th percentile for total behavior-problem score, could be used. This procedure would reduce the proportion of false-positives slightly, at the expense of a large increase in the proportion of false-negatives.

In addition to screening for global maladjustment, it is possible to use Profile scores to identify children manifesting specific behavioral deviations. This procedure is somewhat more time-consuming and results in approximately the same overall error rate as the use of the total behavior-problems score. The advantage of this approach, however, is that once the child has been identified as a positive case, it yields information regarding the specific nature of the disorder the child manifests. Furthermore, procedures are currently available for categorizing children according to their Profile patterns (Edelbrock and Achenbach, 1980). Thus, Profile scores can be used as an aid for both the detection and diagnosis of child psychopathology. The use of discriminant functions to screen children is not recommended, because they are difficult and time-consuming to compute for individual children and do not result in a net improvement in screening efficiency.

Even if there were a perfect screening procedure for detecting child psychopatholgy, several serious problems would remain. Little is known about the prognosis of children's emotional and behavioral disorders without intervention, or what treatments are effective in ameliorating such disorders. Regarding prognosis, some evidence from longitudinal studies indicates that children identified early as maladjusted will continue to manifest significantly more problems than normal controls (Zax et al., 1968; Cowen et al., 1973). The evidence regarding treatment effectiveness, however, is equivocal. In some studies stemming from the

Primary Mental Health Project, children in the treatment groups did not improve more than children in the no-treatment control groups. In fact, on some measures, those in the control groups improved more (Cowen et al., 1975, p. 222). Whereas there is much to be learned regarding the prognosis and appropriate treatments of child psychopathology, refinements in our ability to detect emotional and behavioral deviations are a step toward the construction of comprehensive procedures for the screening, diagnosis, and treatment of child psychopathology.

REFERENCES

Achenbach, T. M. 1978. The Child Behavior Profile: I. Boys aged 6–11. J. Consult. Clin. Psychol. 46, 478–488.

Achenbach, T. M., and Edelbrock, C. S. 1978. The classification of child psychopathology: A review and analysis of empirical efforts. Psychol. Bull. 85, 1275–1301.

Achenbach, T. M., and Edelbrock, C. S. 1979. The Child Behavior Profile: II. Boys aged 12–16 and girls aged 6–11 and 12–16. J. Consult. Clin. Psychol. 47, 223–233.

Achenbach, T. M., and Edelbrock, C. S. 1981. Behavioral Problems and Competencies Reported by Parents of Normal and Disturbed Children Aged 4 Through 16. Monographs of the Society for Research in Child Development.

American Psychiatric Association. 1980. Diagnostic and Statistical Manual of Mental Disorders. 3rd Ed. Washington, D.C. Vol. 46, 1.

Behar, L., and Springfield, S. 1974. A behavior rating scale for the preschool child. Dev. Psychol. 10, 601–610.

Cowen, E. L., Dorr, D., Clarfield, S., Kreling, B., McWilliams, S. A., Pokracki, F., Pratt, D. M., Terrell, D., and Wilson, A. 1973. The AML: A quick screening device for early identification of school maladaptation. Am. J. Commun. Psychol. 1, 12–35.

Cowen, E. L., Pederson, A., Babigan, H., Izzo, L. D., and Trost, M. A. 1973. Long-term follow-up of early detected vulnerable children. J. Consult. Clin. Psychol. 41, 438–446.

Cowen, E. L., Trost, M. A., Lorion, R. P., Dorr, D., Izzo, L. D., and Isaacson, R. V. 1975. New Ways in School Mental Health. Human Sciences Press, New York.

Edelbrock, C., and Achenbach, T. M. 1980. A typology of child behavior profile patterns: Distribution and Correlates for disturbed children aged 6–16. J. Abnorm. Child Psychol. 8, 441–470.

Frankenburg, W. K., and Camp, B. W. (eds.). 1975. Pediatric Screening Tests. Charles C Thomas, Springfield, IL.

Graham, P. 1979. Epidemiological studies. In: H. C. Quay and J. S. Werry (eds.), Psychopathological Disorders of Childhood (2nd ed.) John Wiley & Sons, New York.

Hollingshead, A. B. 1957. Two-factor index of social position. Unpublished manuscript.

Kohn, M., and Rosman, B. L. 1972a. A social competence scale and symptom checklist for the preschool child: Factor dimensions, their cross-instrument generality, and longitudinal persistence. Dev. Psychol. 6, 430–444.

Kohn, M., and Rosman, B. L. 1972b. Prediction of intellectual achievement from preschool social-emotional functioning. Dev. Psychol. 6, 445–452.

Kohn, M., and Rosman, B. L. 1973. A Two-factor model of emotional disturbance in the young child: Validity and screening efficiency. J. Child Psychol. Psychiatry, 14, 31–56.

Langner, T. S., Gersten, J. C., McCarthy, E. D., Eisenberg, J. G., Greene, E. L., Herson, J. H., and Jameson, J. D. 1976. A screening inventory for assessing psychiatric impairment in children 6 to 18. J. Consult. Clin. Psychol. 44, 286–296.

Meehl, P. E., and Rosen, A. 1955. Antecedent probability and the efficiency of psychometric signs, pattern, or cutting scores. Psychol. Bull. 52, 194–216.

O'Leary, K. D., and Johnson, S. B. 1979. Psychological assessment. In: H. C. Quay and J. S. Werry (eds.), Psychopathological Disorders of Childhood. 2nd ed. John Wiley & Sons, New York.

Rutter, M. 1967. A children's behavior questionnaire for completion by teachers: Preliminary findings. J. Child. Psychol. Psychiatry, 8, 1-11.

Zax, M., Cowen, E. L., Rappaport, J., Beach, D. R., and Laird, J. D. 1968. Follow-up study of children identified early as emotionally disturbed. J. Consult. Clin. Psychol. 32, 369–374.

Chapter 7

The HOME Inventory:

A Review of the First Fifteen Years

Robert H. Bradley

Until recently there were few techniques available for accurately and precisely measuring a child's home environment. This is true despite a long-standing consensus among child development specialists that the quality of a child's developmental environment strongly influences the child's growth and development. Prior to 1965, social class or socioeconomic status designations were typically used as indices of adequacy of a child's environment. Because researchers in human development have lacked sensitive measures of environmental quality, progress in understanding how the environment is related to behavior in infants and young children has been slow and uneven. Similarly, child development practitioners have been unable to effectively engineer programs to enhance child development based on specific information about needs and assets in a child's home environment. What is needed are reliable and valid instruments that can assess the stimulation potential of the child's early environment. The intention of this chapter is to describe briefly the development of one such instrument, the Home Observation for Measurement of the Environment (HOME) Inventory, and to review a number of studies that may help clarify its potential usefulness as an assessment tool.

DESCRIPTION OF HOME INVENTORY

Caldwell and her colleagues commenced development of the HOME Inventory in the early 1960s at the Syracuse Early Learning Project (Caldwell and Richmond, 1968). Work has continued on the Inventory at the Center for Child Development and Education in Little Rock, Arkansas.

Currently there are two versions of the HOME Inventory, one for infants (birth to age 3 years) and one for preschoolers (age 3 to 6 years). The instruments designed for assessing the homes of infants contains 45 items clustered in six subscales: 1) emotional and verbal responsivity of mother, 2) avoidance of restriction and punishment, 3) organization of the physical and temporal environment, 4) provision of appropriate play materials, 5) maternal involvement with child, and 6) opportunities for variety in daily stimulation.

Information needed to score items on the Inventory is obtained through a combination of observation and interview. It is administered in the child's home with information supplied by the child's primary caregiver. Administration takes approximately 1 hour, and requires that the child be present and awake. To facilitate scoring, a yes/no format is used. Caldwell and Bradley presented a substantial amount of information regarding the psychometric properties of HOME (Caldwell and Bradley, in press). Examples of items from the six subscales are listed below.

1. *Emotional and verbal responsivity of mother.* Sample item: Mother caresses or kisses child at least once during visit.
2. *Avoidance of restriction and punishment.* Sample item: Mother does not interfere with child's actions or restrict child's movements more than three times during visit.
3. *Organization of physical and temporal environment.* Sample item: Child's play environment appears safe and free of hazards.
4. *Provision of appropriate play materials.* Sample item: Mother provides toys or interesting activities for child during interview.
5. *Maternal involvement with child.* Sample item: Mother tends to keep child within visual range and to look at the child often.
6. *Opportunities for variety in daily stimulation.* Sample item: Child eats at least one meal per day with mother and father.

STUDIES AT THE CENTER FOR
CHILD DEVELOPMENT AND EDUCATION

In 1969, Caldwell and her colleagues at the Center for Child Development and Education, University of Arkansas, Little Rock, inaugurated a longitudinal observation and intervention study examining the relation of home environments and day care to children's development. The participants were quite heterogeneous, albeit the majority were from lower and lower-middle income backgrounds. Approximately 65% of the participants were black.

A series of publications involving this longitudinal study first appeared in 1975. In the first study, 77 children and their families were included (Elardo, Bradley, and Caldwell, 1975). The homes of the children were visited and the HOME Inventory was administered when the children were 6-, 12-, and 24-months-old. The children were also given the Bayley Scales of Infant Development at these points and the Stanford-Binet Intelligence test at age 3. The predictive validity of the Bayley Scales was constrasted with that of the HOME Inventory.

The Mental Development Index (MDI) from the Bayley Scales, measured at age 1, correlated 0.32 ($p < 0.01$) with Binet IQ performance. By contrast, the multiple correlation between HOME subscale scores and 3-year IQ was computed at 0.59 (< 0.01), thus indicating that the HOME is a more effective predictor of IQ than the Bayley.

In a follow-up study, Bradley and Caldwell (1976) found that the strong relation between HOME scores and IQ persisted. The multiple correlation between 6-month HOME scores and 54-month IQ scores was 0.50 ($p < 0.01$); the multiple correlation between 24-month HOME scores and 54-month Binet scores was 0.63 (< 0.01).

Elardo et al. (1977) investigated the relation between HOME scores in the first 2 years of life and language competence as measured by the Illinois Test of Psycholinguistic Abilities (ITPA) at age 3 years. In general, results were like those for IQ scores. Multiple correlations between 2-year HOME scores and 3-year ITPA scores were 0.57 for blacks and 0.74 for whites. In contrast with results for whites, only the 24-month HOME scores were predictive of language competence among blacks. Furthermore, neither organization of the environment nor maternal involvement was as highly correlated with ITPA performance among blacks as whites. Some slight sex differences were also noted, with a stronger relation (nonsignificant) observed for females. Four of the six HOME subscales measured at 24 months showed higher correlations with language for females.

Perhaps the most specifically relevant of studies done at the Center for Child Development and Education from the standpoint of developmental screening was one published by Bradley and Caldwell (1977) dealing with the screening efficiency of the Home Inventory. They assessed the HOME's efficiency in identifying home environments associated with mental retardation and home environments associated with above-average intellectual performance.

A multiple discriminant analysis was used to classify homes as being associated with retarded development (below 70 IQ), below-average development (70–90), and average to above-average development (above 90). Six-month HOME subscales scores were used as predictors, 3-year Binet scores were used as criterion. The discriminant function based on 6-month HOME scores was fairly sensitive in identifying those homes for which the 3-year IQ-test-performance was above average (60% correctly identified). It is important to note that none of the homes having retarded children was classified as being associated with above-average development, and only 18% of those homes having above average children were classified as being associated with retarded development. With regard to identifying those homes associated with retarded development, the specificity of the HOME seems low (43%). There is reason to believe that the high rate of overreferrals results partially from the low base-rate of retardation. Moreover, because 75% of those predicted to have low IQs had Binet scores less than 90, the HOME seems in fact to be identifying children who will not show optimal mental performance. If the HOME was used at age 1, the predictions would likely be even more accurate, given the correlations reported by Elardo et al. (1975). That is, the number of homes incorrectly classified as being associated with retardation (the number of false positives) was high.

In the future, it would be desirable to determine whether equally sensitive predictions would be obtained with less heterogeneous samples, such as one often finds among the client-population of a particular service agency. For example, it might be useful to look at a black sample and a white sample separately to determine if the same level of prediction applies to each.

Recent studies conducted at the Center have sought to delineate more fully the relation between performance on the HOME Inventory and children's development. In one study, Bradley et al. (1977) investigated the relation among home environment. social status, and IQ for 105 children. Their findings showed that the HOME Inventory predicted 3-year IQ scores about as well as the combination of HOME and four SES indices (mother's education, father's education, occupation of head of household, amount of crowding). By comparison, there was generally a loss in predictive power when the SES variables were used by themselves. The most dramatic difference was among a black-only subgroup. In this group, the combination of HOME and SES accounted for almost three times as much variance as did SES alone (34% vs. 12%). The relatively high correlations obtained between HOME and IQ indicate that subtests of HOME are tapping aspects of the early socialization of intelligence in both black and white homes, although the pattern of relations between HOME and IQ seems somewhat different for the two groups. As with ITPA results, correlations between HOME and IQ were higher for females than males (0.79 vs. 0.65).

The final study reported by the Little Rock group was a theoretical investigation of early environmental action. At issue was the observed strong correlation between early experience and later mental-test scores. Do such correlations indicate that early experience has unique salience for cognitive attainment? Alternatively, is the strong relation between early experience and later IQ primarily attributable to the fact that early experience is highly correlated with later experience (i.e., the quality of a child's environment remains stable and it is cumulating experience that makes the difference?) In an effort to examine these alternatives, a series of partial correlations was computed. Six-month HOME scores were correlated with 3-year IQ scores, with 12-month HOME scores partialed out. (See Tables 1 and 2.) Similarly, 12-month HOME scores were correlated with 3-year IQ scores, with 6-month HOME scores partialed out. The results generally indicated that the 6-month HOME scores offered no unique prediction of IQ, whereas the residual correlation between 12-month HOME scores and IQ were significant. Some sex differences were noted in these correlations but most were nonsignificant.

The implications of the study are several. Perhaps the most important is that accurate identification of children at developmental risk stemming from environmental causes requires repeated assessments of the environment. Even though environments generally remain rather stable, in individual cases they may very considerably. Investigations conducted by Honzik, MacFarlane, and Allen (1948) indicated that changes in mental-test performance tend to accompany alterations in the emotional climate of the home.

In summary, studies from the Center for Child Development and Education indicate that the HOME Inventory is a useful assessment tool. A number of additional investigations do need to be undertaken in order

Table 1. Correlations between HOME scores and 36-month IQ

	Time of HOME assessment		
HOME subscales	6 months	12 months	24 months
1. Responsivity	0.25	0.39	0.50
2. Punishment	0.24	0.24	0.41
3. Organization	0.40	0.39	0.41
4. Toys	0.41	0.56	0.64
5. Involvement	0.33	0.47	0.55
6. Variety	0.31	0.28	0.50
Total score	0.50	0.55	0.70
Multiple correlation	0.54	0.59	0.72

Table 2.   Partial correlations between HOME scores and 3-year IQ

HOME subscales	6-month HOME and IQ controlling for 12-month HOME		12-month HOME and IQ controlling for 6-month HOME	
	Male	Female	Male	Female
1. Responsivity	0.07	0.01	0.27	0.49
2. Punishment	0.20	0.03	0.03	0.37
3. Organization	0.25	0.12	0.40	0.46
4. Toys	0.39	0.19	0.61	0.55
5. Involvement	0.05	0.09	0.41	0.53
6. Variety	0.24	0.23	0.19	0.42
Total score	0.21	0.04	0.36	0.53

to understand more fully how the tool can be used. First, there is need to examine more thoroughly the race and sex differences observed. Individual predictions based on information taken from the whole group are not likely to be as accurate as those based on subgroups. Second, there is need to examine the stability of the factor-structure shifts during the birth-to-3-year range; predictions obtained at different age-points may have somewhat different meanings. Third, there is need to examine the predictive efficiency of the HOME when used in combination with other environmental and developmental measures. Some work has already been done in this area. Prediction batteries can be of significant value in large-scale screening programs, such as Child Find and Early and Periodic Screening, Diagnosis and Treatment programs. Fourth, there is need to investigate further the relation of environmental stability to children's development.

STUDIES CONDUCTED BY OTHER RESEARCHERS

In the 15 years since its introduction, the Inventory has enjoyed wide acceptance among both researchers and practitioners. It is currently in use throughout the world and has been translated into several languages. The total number of studies involving the HOME published by other researchers has increased substantially over the last 5 years. Taken together, these studies provide an important complement to those conducted by Caldwell and her colleagues. In these studies, the use of HOME with diverse populations and for various purposes is explored.

One of the earliest explorations of efficiency of the HOME scale as an assessment instrument was reported by Cravioto and DeLicardie (1972). In their longitudinal study involving 229 Mexican infants, extensive environmental, health, and developmental data were gathered on all children. Included were HOME assessments twice yearly up to age 3 years and once again at age 4 years. Of the 229 participating infants, 19 were identified as having experienced severe clinical malnutrition some time prior to age 30 months. After the 19 index cases of malnutrition had been identified, Cravioto and DeLicardie selected from the remaining 210 children a matched sample of 19 children for a comparison group. Matching was on the basis of parental education, literacy, personal cleanliness, family size, and socioeconomic status. The investigators examined the 6-month HOME scores of the two groups. The results indicated that the children who developed malnutrition were living at age 6-months in homes much lower in stimulation and support for development than were matched-comparison children. When the homes were assessed again at 48 months, the picture was essentially the same.

In a related study, the HOME Inventory (73-item version) was employed in the Chase and Martin (1970) study of undernutrition and child development. Nineteen children with a primary diagnosis of generalized undernutrition provided the chief focus of the investigation. The mean HOME scores of these children was six points lower than the mean HOME scores of 19 control children from similar SES backgrounds. Such findings corroborate those reported by Cravioto and DeLicardie (1972). In general, the environmental characteristics measured seem to provide a kind of early warning system for the eventual development of malnourishment. Moreover, the findings provide evidence that the environmental processes included in Home are associated with a pattern of caregiving required for a variety of health and development outcomes.

The Stanislawski (1977) investigation represents another attempt to evaluate the efficiency of the HOME scale in identifying children at developmental risk. More specifically, Stanislawski explored the ability of the HOME Inventory to discriminate among populations of children (developmentally disabled, developmentally delayed, and developmentally normal). The developmentally disabled group included children whose developmental problems were attributable to neurological factors. The developmentally delayed group included children whose problems did not seem to result from physical conditions. Participants were 42 mother-child dyads divided into groups determined by the child's developmental status. Results showed that the HOME scale differentiated between the environments of delayed children and the environments of the other two groups ($p < 0.05$). The mean score for the delayed group was 32.7 as compared to means of about 40 for the other groups.

Van Doorninck et al. (1977) completed a long-term study of the HOME Inventory that involved children from the Syracuse Early Learning Project (Caldwell and Richmond, 1968). They found that 43% of the children from lower-class families had school problems, including low scores on achievement tests, low grades, and poor performance in reading and mathematics. Only 7% of parents of higher socioeconomic status had children with such school problems. This selection procedure, however, included a large number of low-SES children who did well in school. In their sample, 56% of the low-SES children had no reported school problems. These low-SES and high-achievement families would have been needlessly identified and "assisted" with supplemental programs. The investigators noted that the overinclusion of the low-SES children in the high-risk group could have been avoided to a large extent if HOME scores had been employed to classify children at risk, because the overreferral rate with HOME was just 33%.

Another study that provided information on the utility of the HOME scale as an assessment instrument was conducted by Hayes (1977). This investigation of the effects of environmental stimulation on premature infants included 17 premature infants who received various forms of visual and tactile stimulation during the weeks immediately after birth, 14 premature infants who received no special enrichment stimulation, and 16 full-term infants. Performance on the McCarthy Scales of Children's Abilities was used as an index of the children's cognitive capability. A higher score on the HOME was related to higher developmental scores within all three groups, albeit results differed somewhat from group to group. Among the HOME subscores, Avoidance of Restriction and Punishment showed the highest correlation with infant cognitive ability. Interestingly, when the HOME scores and the infants' Apgar scores were combined to predict competence, HOME was by far the better predictor. Findings from the study indicate that HOME is a good predictor of development among premature infants. Additionally, it was noted that certain features of the environment (Avoidance of Restriction and Punishment) may be more salient for development within this group than for full-term infants.

One of the better studies aimed at determining the ability of the HOME to identify home environments associated with poor development was conducted by Wulbert et al. (1975). These researchers identified a group of preschool children who had delayed language development but who showed a high probability of normal intelligence. Probable normal intelligence was defined in terms of having a much higher score on the Leiter International Performance Scale than on the Stanford-Binet Intelligence Test. The average difference was slightly in excess of 20 points in favor of the Leiter nonverbal measure. The home environments of these language-delayed children were compared to the home environments of normal children and to those of children with developmental disabilities for which psychosocial causation would not be suspected. For this third group, children with Down's syndrome were chosen. Results of the study revealed that the children with language disabilities did in fact live in home environments that differed markedly from those of the normal and Down's syndrome children. More specifically, an analysis of variance showed that the mean score of the language-disability group was significantly lower on five of the six HOME subscales.

Ramey et al. (1975) compared the stimulation available in the homes of infants thought to be at risk for socioculturally-determined developmental retardation with the stimulation available to a contrast group drawn from the general population. Their operational definition of high-risk group involved lower family income, lower parental educational and intelligence levels, and higher density within the home, that is, more crowding. The findings are striking in that the homes thought to be potentially-high contributors to the developmentally-retarded population, as a function of a broad variety of family structure and status characteristics, recorded significantly lower on all of the six HOME subscales when compared to the homes of infants from the general population. It seems therefore that HOME identifies many of the day-to-day events and transactions that distinguish advantaged and disadvantaged homes.

Among the more recent studies investigating the predictability of the HOME Inventory is one reported by Piper and Ramsay (1980) involving 37 Down's syndrome infants. The infants were followed for a 6-month period (mean age at entry = 8.9 months). Changes in their mental development over this period, as measured by the Griffiths Mental Developmental Scales, were correlated with initial scores on the HOME Inventory. Results showed that three HOME subscales—Organization of the Physical and Temporal Environment, Opportunities for Variety in Daily Stimulation, and Maternal Involvement with Child—were significantly related to the Griffiths Personal-Social Scale. A discriminant analysis composed of these three subscales differentiated the infants into two groups according to the degree of decline in their total Griffiths score. The minimal-decline group was associated with a better organization of the environment.

In addition to the studies dealing with the screening ability of the HOME Inventory, a number of others have appeared that examine the association between HOME scores and aspects of cognitive development. For example, Fowler and his colleagues (Fowler, 1978; Fowler and Swenson, 1975) conducted a longitudinal study of 23 day-care children and 23 matched home-reared children living in Toronto, Canada. The study began when the children were 6 months old and continued until they were about 5½ years old. A majority of the children were from single-parent families and most were either lower SES or lower-middle SES. The children were assessed with the Griffiths Scale, the

Schaefer-Aaronson Behavior Rating Scale, and the Stanford-Binet Intelligence Test. Correlations between HOME scores and scores on these measures of cognitive and social development ranged from moderate to strong (0.4–0.8). The coefficients varied as a function of the age at which the child was measured. HOME scores generally showed a stronger relation to verbal factors than to affective or perceptual-motor factors.

In a sophisticated investigation of environmental effects of educational and cognitive attainment, Jordan (1976) used three means of assessing environmental quality: SES, the HOME Inventory, and the Coddington Scale. The Coddington Life Change Events Scale (1972) measures the amount of change in a child's life. Changes in a child's life, such as divorce of parents, parents' loss of job, and moving, are recorded on the scale. These events are then translated into "life change units," with some events assigned greater weight than others. Theoretically, changes in life produce stress for the individual because they require the person to adapt in order to cope with the changes. At age 5, the 165 St. Louis children who took part in the longitudinal study were also assessed with the Wide Range Achievement Test (WRAT) reading subtest and the Raven's Coloured Progressive Matrices, a nonverbal measure of cognitive capability. An interaction regression procedure was used to examine how the various components of the child's environment interacted to affect performance on the two outcome measures. All three environmental measures showed strong relations with cognitive performance. Perhaps more important, interactions were observed between the three environmental measures in terms of their effect on cognitive competence. Certain aspects of the environment seemed significantly related to the criterion-developmental measures only when certain other environmental measures reached a particular level. To be more specific, the WRAT scores of children with low SES were significantly related to the HOME scores.

A second analysis by Jordan (1978) examined the relation of language competence and various environmental measures. The language competence of 181 children was assessed at age 5 with the Vocabulary section of the Wechsler Preschool and Primary Scale of Intelligence. Environmental factors included SES, family structure measures, assessments of home conditions, and HOME scale. Based on results of an interaction regression analysis, Jordan concluded that "the pattern of elements within homes (especially the HOME scores) exerts an influence on language development greater than that of any other factor in the complex of influences chosen for the study."

Johnson et al. (1976) studied three cohorts of Mexican-American children from the Houston Parent-Child Center. In two of the cohorts, children who received intervention showed higher HOME scores than did control children. Among these children, HOME scores were correlated significantly with 24-month Bayley Mental Development Index (0.4) and 36-month IQ (0.5–0.7).

HOME has been used successfully in a variety of settings outside the United States, including Canada, Mexico, Guatemala, England, Japan, and Argentina. Moreover, it has been used with a variety of ethnic groups within the United States, including whites, blacks, Mexican-Americans, and other Spanish-speaking Americans. It has been used effectively in urban, surburban, and rural settings, and has been employed with children with special problems, including Down's syndrome, low birthweight, language impairment, and drug dependency. In many of the situations, HOME scores demonstrated an important relation to health and development outcomes, albeit the strength of the relation was not uniform across groups. It seems particularly significant that in several studies involving children with developmental delays, HOME was able to discriminate between groups in which the primary suspected cause of delay was environmental and groups in which the primary suspected cause was organismic. Moreover, it is significant that HOME seems to provide reasonably accurate prognosis for intellectual attainment among several specialized groups (e.g., low birthweight, Down's syndrome) as well as among groups not at medical risk.

In summary, the studies reviewed present a consistent profile with respect to the HOME Inventory: it can be useful in identifying children at risk for developmental delay. This conclusion is drawn from studies wherein significant correlations between HOME scores and developmental measures were observed. It also follows from studies wherein HOME was shown to discriminate between children for whom organismic causation was suspected as the basic for developmental delay and children for whom environmental causation was suspected. More generally, the studies reviewed, especially those dealing with malnutrition and with drug dependency, seem to indicate that HOME is tapping a constellation of family environment variables salient for a broad array of health and development outcomes. It seems likely that the processes are among those implicated among such groups as "failure-to-thrive" and abuse. The most often observed findings are those involving mental test and language scores, albeit social and health variables have also been shown to be related to HOME scores. Frequently absent in the studies reviewed are explorations of sex differences. Given findings by Bradley et al. (1977) and Bradley and Caldwell (1980) that reveal sex differences, such examinations are critical. It also seems important to conduct additional investigations of the relation of HOME and development scores within restricted socioeconomic groups. In one such study, Stevenson and Lamb (1979) concluded that the HOME scale was too insensitive to reveal differences among middle class homes.

EPILOGUE: REFLECTIONS OF A HOME FUTUROLOGIST

Review of the burgeoning research on the HOME Inventory suggests a number of potentially fruitful research activities on environmental measurement. First, there is need for carefully conducted crosscultural studies, both to examine applicability of the HOME in various milieus and to form the basis for a theory of environment/development relationships. Second, there is need to pool existing data from large projects that have collected HOME data as part of their ongoing research and service activities. Such pooling would allow the development of more adequate norms, the use of statistical procedures for which large data sets are necessary, the comparison of environment/development relations across different populations, and more appropriate testing of certain psychometric properties of the instrument. Third, there is need to examine the stability of HOME scores on how such stability affects development. Fourth, there is need to investigate more thoroughly relations between HOME scores and socioemotional outcomes. (A recent useful study in this area was conducted by Bakeman and Brown (1980). Their study of 43 black dyads revealed that social competence at age 3 was related to the Emotional and Verbal Responsivity subscale of the HOME as measured when the infants were 20 months old.) Fifth, there is need to develop specific predictive equations using HOME for various specialized groups, (e.g., single parent, handicapped, low birthweight, parents with severe mental health problems).

In general, the HOME seems to be a useful assessment device. The future for research with the instrument is open and alluring. Among the challenges is the development of theory relating environment to development. Such theory would lead to substantial improvements in the instrument and its applications.

REFERENCES

Bakeman, R., and Brown, J. 1980. Early interaction: Consequences for social and mental development at three years. Child Dev. 51:437–447.
Bradley, R., and Caldwell, B. 1980. The relation of home environment, cognitive competence, and IQ among males and females. Child Dev. 51:1140–1148.
Bradley, R., and Caldwell, B. 1977. Home observaton for measurement of the environment: A validation study of screening efficiency. Am. J. Ment. Defic., 81:417–420.

Bradley, R., and Caldwell, B. 1976. Early home environment and changes in mental test performance in children from six to thirty-six months. Dev. Psychol. 12:93–97.

Bradley, R., and Caldwell, B. 1976. The relationship of infants' home environments to mental test performance at fifty-four months: A follow-up study. Child Dev. 47:1172–1174.

Bradley, R., Caldwell, B., and Elardo, R. 1979. Home environment and cognitive development in the first two years of life: a cross-lagged panel analysis. Dev. Psychol. 15:246–250.

Bradley, R., Caldwell, B., and Elardo, R. 1977. Home environment, social status and mental test performance. J. Educ. Psychol. 69:697–701.

Caldwell, B., and Bradley, R. Home Observation for Measurement of the Environment. Dorsey Press, New York. In press.

Caldwell, B., and Richmond, J. 1968. The children's center in Syracuse, New York. In: L. D. Hman (ed.), Early Child Care: The New Perspectives. Atherton, New York.

Chase, H., and Martin, H. 1970. Undernutrition and child development. New England J. Med. 282:933–939.

Coddington, R. 1972. The significance of life events as etiologic factors in the diseases of children, II: A study of a normal population. J. Psychosomatic Res. 16:205–213.

Cravioto, J., and DeLicardie, E. 1972. Environmental correlates of severe clinical malnutrition and language development in survivors of Kwashiorkor or Marasmus. In: Nutrition: The Nervous System and Behavior. Scientific Publication No. 251, Pan-American Health Organization, Washington, D.C.

Elardo, R., Bradley, R., and Caldwell, B. 1977. A longitudinal study of the relation of infants' home environments to language development at age three. Child Dev. 48:595–603.

Elardo, R., Bradley, R., and Caldwell, B. 1975. The relation of infants' home environments to mental test performance from six to thirty-six months: A longitudinal analysis. Child Dev. 46:71–76.

Fowler, W. 1978. Day Care and Its Effects on Early Development. Ontario Institute for Studies in Education, Research in Education Series, #8, Toronto.

Fowler, W., and Swenson, A. 1975. The Influence of Early Stimulation on Language Development. Ontario Institute for Studies in Education, Department of Applied Psychology, Toronto.

Havighurst, R. 1976. The relative importance of social class and ethnicity in human development. Human Dev. 19:56–64.

Hayes, J. Premature infant development: An investigation of the relationship of neonatal stimulation, birth condition and home environment to development at age three years. Unpublished doctoral dissertation, Purdue University, 1977.

Honzik, M., MacFarlane, J., and Allen, L. 1948. The stability of mental test performance between two and eighteen years. J. Exp. Educ. 18:309–324.

Johnson, D., Kahn, A., Hines, R., Leler, H. and Torres, M. Measuring the learning environment of Mexican-American families in a parent education program. Paper presented at the annual meeting of the American Educational Research Association, San Francisco, Cal. 1976.

Jordan, T. 1978. Influences on vocabulary attainment: A five-year prospective study. Child Dev. 49:1096–1106.

Jordan, T. Measurement of learning and its effects on cognitive and educational attainment. Paper presented at the annual meeting of the American Educational Research Association, San Francisco, Cal. 1976.

Lytton, H. 1971. Observation studies of parent-child interaction: A methodological review. Child Dev. 42:651–684.

Piper, M., and Ramsay, M. 1980. Effects of early home environment on the mental development of Down syndrome infants. Am. J. Ment. Defic. 85:39–44.

Ramey, C., Mills, P., Campbell, F., and O'Brien, C. 1975. Infants' home environments: A comparison of high-risk families and families from the general population. Am J. Ment. Defic. 80:40–42.

Stanislawski, E. A comparison of the DDST and HOME for developmental assessment with three populations of young children. Unpublished master's thesis, University of Wisconsin, 1977.

Stevenson, M., and Lamb, M. 1979. Effects of infant sociability and the caretaking environment on infant cognitive performance. Child Dev. 50:340–349.

van Doorninck, W., Caldwell, B., Wright, C., and Frankenburg, W. The relationship between the 12-month inventory of home stimulation and school competence. Paper presented at the biennial meeting of the Society for Research in Child Development, Denver, Col. 1977.

Wulbert, M., Inglis, S., Kriegsmann, E., and Mills, B. 1975. Language delay and associated mother-child interactions. Dev. Psychol. 2:61–70.

Chapter 8

Preliminary Results of a Combined Developmental/ Environmental Screening Project

Cecilia E. Coons, William K. Frankenburg, Elizabeth C. Gay, Alma W. Fandal, Dianne L. Lefly, Cynthia Ker

The research staff of the John F. Kennedy Child Development Center, Denver, Colorado, has been engaged in research directed at improving developmental screening instruments in order to identify young children who are handicapped or at risk of experiencing later school problems. Such efforts led to the Denver Developmental Screening Test (DDST), which is used in many health settings throughout the United States and has been or is being standardized in approximately eight other countries. Nonnormal scores on the DDST are highly predictive of later school problems. As is true with most developmental tests, however, normal scores are not highly predictive of school success. A relatively large number of children who seem to be developing normally during their early years go on to fail or to experience severe school problems. The failure of traditional developmental tests to identify these children is most likely attributable to one or more of the following reasons:

1. There may be errors inherent in the test itself.
2. The child may be developing normally at the time the test is administered, but factors in the environment negatively affect the child's normal course of development.

3.   The child's difficulties in school may be attributable to factors within the school setting (such as the teacher's personality or inappropriate expectations), which could not have been predicted through screening.

Test developers have addressed the first cause of predictive errors by conducting studies to revise some of the developmental diagnostic tests, including the Wechsler Intelligence Scales for Children, the Stanford-Binet Intelligence Test, and screening tests such as the DDST. These efforts have met with limited success.

Few studies have been done that address the second reason for predictive errors—influential factors in the child's early environment. A major study was therefore initiated 3 years ago to develop the Home Screening Questionnaire (HSQ), an instrument for screening the young child's early home environment, and to evaluate the accuracy of a combined developmental/environmental screening process. The purpose of this chapter is to describe the study and to report results on the characteristics of the HSQ.

THE PROJECT

The project consisted essentially of three phases. In Phase I, the Home Screening Questionnaire (HSQ) was developed for children of two age groups, 0–3 years and 3–6 years. Bettye Caldwell's Home Observation for Measurement of the Environment Inventory (HOME) was used as a guide for developing the HSQ (Caldwell and Bradley, 1978).

In Phase II, a larger number of children in the Denver metropolitan area were screened with the HSQ and the DDST. A subsample of these children was followed up with the HOME Inventory. In Phase III, school records of siblings of children screened in Phase II were evaluated as an initial or cursory estimate of test validity. The procedures used in each of these phases are described briefly before the results are presented.

Phase I

In Phase I, items were selected from the HOME Inventory and reconstructed into questionnaire format. Two questionnaires were developed to correspond to the two HOME scales (i.e., for children from birth to 3 years and from 3 to 6 years of age). Parents of approximately 50 children in each age group were asked to complete the HSQ for their children while waiting to be seen in a Denver public health clinic. A follow-up home visit using the HOME Inventory was completed approximately 2 weeks later. Item and total score analyses were done to compare the HSQ and HOME, and revisions were made on the HSQ to improve agreement with the HOME scales. This procedure was repeated twice. The final total score correlations between the HSQ and HOME at the end of Phase I were 0.71 (N = 61) for the 0–3 years form and 0.81 (N = 58) for the 3–6 years form.

The 0–3 years HSQ consists of 30 items plus a checklist of toys available to the child in the home. The 3–6 years HSQ consists of 34 items and a similar toy checklist. The HSQs are written at approximately a third or fourth grade reading level and require 15 to 20 minutes to complete. Both HSQ forms consist of multiple-choice, fill-in-the-blank, and Yes/No questions. Sample questions are shown in Figure 1.

Phase II

In Phase II, 1,365 children in Denver public health clinics or Head Start Centers serving low-income families were screened with the HSQ and the DDST. There were 868 children in the 0–3 group and 497 in the 3–6 group. Follow-up HOME interviews were conducted on 790 of the children screened—503 in the 0–3 group and 287 in the 3–6 group. Only children in low socioeconomic environments were included because previous studies have shown that the HOME Inventory does not discriminate in middle- and upper-income populations (Stevenson and Lamb, 1979), and because the rate of school problems is highest in the low-income population (van Doorninck, 1978).

In the 0–3 sample, approximately 62% of the children were Anglo, 4% were black, 25% were Hispanic, and 9% were either mixed or of other ethnic backgrounds. In the 3–6 sample, approximately 41% were Anglo, 8% were black, 43% were Hispanic, and 8% were either mixed or of other ethnic backgrounds. There was a slightly higher percent of Hispanics and a lower percent of blacks in this sample than in the Denver population. There was an almost equal number of males and females in both samples.

For both age groups, approximately 41% of the mothers and 35% of the fathers had had less than high school education, 44% of the

How many children's books does your child have of his or her *own*?

_____ 0—too young
_____ 1 or 2
_____ 3 to 9
_____ 10 or more

About how often do you take your child to the doctor?

Do you have any friends with children about the same age as your child?

_____ Yes
_____ No

Figure 1. Sample questions from HSQ.

mothers and 40% of the fathers had completed high school, 12% of the mothers and 16% of the fathers had had some college education, and 3% of the mothers and 9% of the fathers had completed college.

Screening was done by project staff and by screeners already employed by the public health clinics. All screeners were required to pass the DDST proficiency exam prior to screening children in Phase II. Throughout this 2-year data collection phase, nine interviewers were trained to administer the HOME scale. In addition, Robert Bradley, a co-author of the HOME scales, consulted with the staff and answered questions regarding specific HOME items and interviewing techniques. Each interviewer was required to obtain at least 90% administration and scoring agreement with a trained interviewer on two consecutive HOME interviews for each of the two age groups of children. To further ensure adequate interobserver and interscorer reliability, interviewers obtained at least 90% administration and scoring agreement with at least two other interviewers on the staff. These precautions were taken because of the possibility of increased error due to the use of multiple interviewers.

Phase III

In Phase III, sibling school status was obtained as a gross estimate of concurrent test validity. The use of sibling outcome measures has been recommended by Hunt (1979) and employed in previous studies by White and Watts (1973) because the environments of these children are generally quite similar. The authors of this project plan to conduct a final and finite validation study on the children who were screened once they have entered school.

Phase III was conducted simultaneously with Phase II. School records of siblings were reviewed, and school performance of each sibling was classified into one of two categories, "school problems" or "no school problems." Based on a school follow-up study by van Doorninck (1978) and on recommendations from John Lampe, Chief of Health and Social Services for the Denver Public Schools, one or more of the following conditions was classified as a school problem:

Institutionalization
Special placement (i.e., emotionally handicapped or disturbed, mentally retarded, speech and hearing problems
One or more grades repeated
Score on national achievement test below the 10th percentile
Failure in core subjects
Repeated concerns by teachers

Sufficient school data were available to determine school status of 191 of the 211 siblings whose school records were reviewed. Fifty-one percent of siblings of children in the 0–3 group and 58% of siblings of children in the 3–6 group were experiencing school problems. These percentages approximate the rate of school problems in disadvantaged environments reported by van Doorninck (1978) and Werner, Bierman, and French (1971).

RELIABILITY AND VALIDITY

Analyses were done to determine the reliability of the newly developed HSQ. Internal reliability coefficients for both HSQ forms were calculated using the Kuder-Richardson Formula 20. These coefficients are 0.73 ($N = 868$) for the 0–3 HSQ and 0.80 ($N = 497$) for the 3–6 HSQ. Throughout the data collection phase, a few parents were asked to complete a second HSQ after an interval of a few weeks rather than participating in the HOME interview, in order to allow calculation of test-retest reliability. The number of test-retest HSQs available to date is small, but more are to be collected within the next few months. The test-retest reliability coefficients are 0.61 ($N = 20$) for the 0–3 HSQ and 0.86 ($N = 16$) for the 3–6 HSQ. The average time between tests was approximately 1 month for the 0–3 group and 4 months for the 3–6 group.

To evaluate the validity of the HSQs and HOMEs in identifying sibling school status, it was first necessary to select cutoff scores that would separate positive from negative test results. Cross tabulations were run showing school outcome (i.e., problems versus no problems) at each HOME and HSQ cutoff score for both age groups. Scores that resulted in the lowest overall errors (i.e., overreferrals, or false positives, combined with underreferrals, or false negatives) were selected as HSQ or HOME inventory cutoff scores for this study.

Using these cutoff scores, analyses were done to evaluate the accuracy of the DDST, the HSQ, and the HOME in identifying sibling school problems. This was also done for the DDST/HSQ and DDST/HOME combinations.

Results

Table 1 summarizes the results of the analyses for the 0–3 years age group. DDST results were a poor predictor of sibling school status. This is understandable because the DDST measures development largely affected by the child's own biological integrity, not that of a sibling. Selecting the 0–3 HOME cutoff score on the basis of minimizing errors

Table 1.   Validity estimates (sibling school status) for the 0–3 years group

Measure	Sensitivity (%)	Specificity (%)	Overreferrals (%)	Underreferals (%)
DDST	5	98	1	49
HOME	61	72	14	19
HSQ	81	38	30	10
HOME/DDST	61	69	16	19
HSQ/DDST	83	38	31	9

Sensitivity = accuracy in identifying "problems."
Specificity = accuracy in identifying "no problems."
Overreferrals = false positives.
Underreferrals = false negatives.

resulted in a sensitivity rate of 61%. This means that low scores on the HOME Inventory identified 61% of all sibling school problems. When the 0–3 HSQ cutoff score was selected on the basis of minimizing errors, the sensitivity was 81%. The specificity, or accuracy in identifying siblings who were not experiencing school problems was 72% for the 0–3 HOME Inventory and 38% for the 0–3 HSQ. The difference between HSQ and HOME specificity rates was statistically significant at the 0.05 probability level, but the difference between the sensitivity rates did not reach significance. Overreferrals, or false positives, are errors in which the test result is positive (suspect), but the true status of the individual is normal. Underreferrals, or false negatives, are errors in which the test result is negative (nonsuspect), but the true status of the individual is nonnormal. Overreferral and underreferral rates can be calculated one of two ways: as a percentage of children referred, or as a percentage of the total sample. Rates shown here were calculated on the total sample.

For the 0–3 group, the rate of overreferrals was 14% for the HOME Inventory and 30% for the HSQ. The rate of underreferrals was 19% for the HOME Inventory and 10% for the HSQ.

The DDST did not add significantly to the prediction of sibling problems when used in conjunction with the HSQ or HOME. This finding was not surprising given the low sensitivity for the DDST alone. The 0–3 HOME Inventory produced significantly fewer overreferral errors than did the 0–3 HSQ ($p < 0.05$). Overreferrals were the major source of error in the HSQ. Sensitivity, specificity, overreferral, and underreferral rates can all be changed by altering the test cutoff score. It should be emphasized, however, that cutoff scores were selected by minimizing overall errors. This means that any attempt to improve sensitivity or specificity will be accompanied by an increase in the overall error rate.

Various factors, such as the intent of the instrument and the effects associated with each type of error, must be considered when establishing scoring recommendations for a test. Because the HSQ is a screening instrument requiring only 15 to 20 minutes of the parent's time to complete, an overreferral rate higher than that obtained with a diagnostic test might be tolerated. It is important to remember that these results were based on sibling school outcomes. It is anticipated that the results will improve for children actually screened.

Table 2 shows results for the 3–6 form. Again, the DDST was a poor indicator of sibling school problems. The sensitivities for both the HSQ and HOME were high for the 3–6 group. The HOME Inventory identified 79% of sibling school problems and the HSQ identified 81% of the problems. Although the specificity rates for both instruments were relatively low, these are screening instruments, and their goal is to identify children at risk for problems. Therefore, a low specificity is more tolerable if sensitivity is increased. With a diagnostic instrument, it is important to increase specificity because referrals are based on diagnostic results. Results for the 3–6 HSQ were highly comparable to the results for the 3–6 HOME. There were no statistically significant differences in any of the measures. Similar to the results for the 0–3 group, the DDST did not increase the prediction of sibling school problems beyond that obtained by the HSQ or HOME Inventory used alone. Again, it is important to remember that these results are based on sibling school performance.

These preliminary results suggest that the HSQ may be an accurate and cost-efficient screening instrument of the home environment for children from birth to 6 years of age.

DISCUSSION

In conclusion, the findings suggest the following:

1. The correlation between the HSQ and HOME Inventory is relatively high. The HSQ, a parent-answered questionnaire, is a more eco-

Table 2.   Validity estimates (sibling school status) for the 3–6 year group

Measure	Sensitivity (%)	Specificity (%)	Overreferrals (%)	Underreferals (%)
DDST	29	83	7	41
HOME	79	34	25	13
HSQ	81	41	25	11
HOME/DDST	87	31	26	8
HSQ/DDST	86	41	25	8

Sensitivity = accuracy in identifying "problems."
Specificity = accuracy in identifying "no problems."
Overreferrals = false positives.
Underreferrals = false negatives.

nomical approach to screening the home environment than is the HOME Inventory.

2. Comparison of both the 0–3 and 3–6 forms of the HSQ to sibling school performance indicates that both forms of the HSQ are equally accurate. In addition, they are as accurate as the HOME Inventory in identifying school problems (although the 0–3 HOME Inventory predicted "no problems" significantly better than the 0–3 HSQ; see Specificity in Table 1). It is important to recognize that these results are for siblings. The home environment probably would have fairly similar effects upon school performance of siblings, but the environment does change from time to time and may differ in important aspects for siblings.

3. DDST results are not highly predictive of sibling school performance. The sensitivities are only 5% for the 0–3 group of siblings and 29% for the 3–6 group of siblings. This finding is not surprising because only about 12%–15% of children obtain nonnormal DDST results, whereas the rate of school problems is approximately 50%. The higher DDST sensitivity for the 3–6-year-olds may be attributable to one or more factors:

    a. a higher prevalence of nonnormal DDSTS for this age group.
    b. A shorter time span between screening and sibling assessment than for the 0–3 group, and
    c. the fact that the DDST measures a child's performance, which in turn is dependent upon the child's biological integrity and experience. These experiences for the infant and preschooler are markedly influenced by the home environment, which seems to be reflected in DDST scores starting at about 2 years of age. Thus, for 3–6-year-olds, a greater portion of the child's score reflects the home environment, and it is this environment that may be strongly influencing the sibling's school performance.

Figure 2 schematically shows the relative proportion of biological and environmental factors that determines developmental status from birth to 6 years. It is the recognition of these factors determining later school performance that prompted the authors to combine an environmental screen and a developmental screen to increase the sensitivity in predicting later school problems.

A follow-up of the children screened will be required to determine the success of this effort, because the purpose of the research is to determine predictive accuracy of the screened child, not of the sibling. A study of this type has been proposed, which will determine the most precise way of scoring the HSQs and the DDST in predicting later school problems.

Total developmental performance

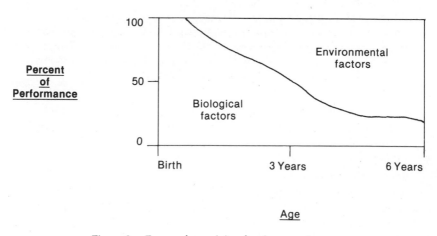

Figure 2.   Factors determining developmental status.

In evaluating their screening approaches, the authors recognize these limitations:

1. The child and his or her environment constantly interact and change each other over time (it is a transactional process).
2. School failure is a symptom that can be attributed to a variety of factors, many of which are not evaluated by either the DDST or the HSQ.

Nevertheless, a combined application of the simple and relatively inexpensive DDST and HSQ to low SES children should identify early a certain proportion of children having a high probability of later school failure. Attempts can then be made to provide these children and their families with specific services to prevent later school failure. It is the authors' view that the selectivity of such an approach would be far more efficient and less costly than the current position: that all children residing in poverty need early intervention, as exemplified by Head Start. It should be remembered that approximately 50% of children living in poverty do not fail in school. Therefore, the available funds for child programs would be more profitably spent if they could be directed early to the 50% of children who are most in need of such programs.

REFERENCES

Caldwell, B. M., and Bradley, R. 1978. Home Observation for Measurement of the Environment (manual). University of Arkansas Press, Little Rock.

Hunt, J. M. 1979. Longitudinal research: A method for the study of development of high risk pre-term infants. In: T. Field (ed.), Infants Born At Risk, Part VII, Methodological Issues, pp. 443–459. Spectrum Publications, New York.

Stevenson, M., and Lamb, M. 1979. Effects of infant sociability and the caretaking environment on infant cognitive performance. Child Dev. 50:340–349.

van Doorninck, W. J. 1978. Prediction of school performance from infant and preschool developmental screening. In: W. K. Frankenburg (ed.), Proceedings of the Second International Conference on Developmental Screening, pp. 163–172. University of Colorado Medical Center Press, Denver.

Werner, E. E., Bierman, J. M., and French, F. E. 1971. The Children of Kauai. University of Hawaii Press, Honolulu.

White, B. L., and Watts, J. 1973. Experience and Environment: Major Influences on the Development of the Young Child. Vol. I. Prentice-Hall, Englewood Cliffs, NJ.

Chapter 9

Early Detection of Developmental Problems by Questionnaire, Interview, and Observation

A. T. M. Cools

For about 10 years the research project, Early Detection of Children with Developmental Problems, has taken place in Utrecht, Holland. This project led to the standardization of the Denver Ontwikkeling Screening test (DOS), the Dutch adaptation of the Denver Developmental Screening Test. The reliability, validity, and efficiency of the DOS have since been tested within the structure of the Dutch Public Health Service. Further research has been done on the possibilities of increasing both the efficiency and accuracy of the DOS as a screening procedure to identify developmental delays in young children. This chapter presents an account of two such projects.

PROBLEM

Past research on the efficiency of the DOS revealed that of all of the children screened with the DOS, only 3% to 9% had developmental problems. This means that when using the DOS, a great many children have to be tested and much energy is spent in order to identify relatively few children. Such findings evoke the question, Is it justified to screen such a large sample of children to identify a small group of children with developmental problems? It should be considered that testing may cause emotional strains, both in the children and their parents, and it may also raise the danger of an unjustified stigma for the children. Economic concerns may also contribute to the problems of screening. Thus, it was decided to investigate whether a number of children might be spared the screening test by the use of a more simple procedure. Analogous to the research of Frankenburg and his team in Denver (Frankenburg et al., 1976b), it was decided to investigate whether and to what extent it might be possible to use a short, parent-answered questionnaire to identify those children who demonstrate no developmental problems. The decision of whether a DOS would be given to a child could then be based on the results of the parent questionnaire.

The validity of the DOS presented another problem. A number of children who had nonnormal DOS results appeared in clinical diagnoses to be false positives. The question that arose was whether the screening procedure could be improved and refined with the aid of verbal and nonverbal information from the parents, thus making the DOS more precise and minimizing the number of false positives.

THE QUESTIONNAIRE

Construction of the Questionnaire

Before constructing a questionnaire, the decision had to be made as to which age group or groups would be concerned. The strategy of covering all ages between 0 and 6 years had been applied by Frankenburg and his team. The result, however, was a rather complicated instrument of overlapping scales. Another possibility was that of constructing a limited number of questionnaires for specific ages. The latter was chosen, partly for pragmatic reasons.

In a longitudinal study of the validity of the DOS, which began in 1975 (Cools and Hermanns, 1977, 1979), it was determined to what extent the DOS could be applied in a justified manner for a number of exactly defined age groups (i.e., 7 weeks, 6 months, 10 months, 1½ years, 2¼ years). It was possible to include in this validation study a preliminary investigaton of a parent-answered questionnaire for each of these age groups except 7 weeks. The 6-months age group was dropped after an explorative investigation, and this report does not include the results of a questionnaire for that age group.

Once the ages to be covered by the questionnaire were determined, it was necessary to select the questions to be used for each age group. Items selected from the DOS were written in the form of questions so that parents could easily answer each one "yes" or "no." Criteria for item selection were: ease of scoring; that the behavior being tested was easily recognized by the parent; and that no additional material was needed to understand or administer the item. The items used on the initial questionnaires had been scored positively by 90% of the children tested during the standardization of the DOS and were as close as possible to the designated age for a specific questionnaire. In pilot studies, however, so many parents answered those questions positively that there was little discrimination among groups on these items. Thus, a selection of items was expanded to include some items that had been scored positively by less than 90% of the DOS standardization sample.

A major attempt was made to limit the number of questions so that the parents' concentration and motivation should not be overtaxed. Because more DOS items need to be administered as a child grows older, the parent questionnaires for the 1½ years and 2¼ years reflect this change and include 12 and 16 questions, respectively, rather than the 10 that are on the questionnaire for the 10-months age group. Finally, a short introduction was written in which the object of the questionnaire and directions for filling it in were explained; it also reassured parents that the child, to be normally developing, need not be able to do all tasks.

Procedure

As mentioned above, the initial validity research on the questionnaires was done within the longitudinal investigation of the validity of the DOS, which was carried out in Hoogeveen. A second investigation to contravalidate the first study was conducted in Utrecht. As a result of these studies, questionnaires were validated for children aged 10 months, 1½ years, and 2¼ years.

Results and Discussion

In discussing the results, four major points can be made. First, the results of both investigations (Hoogeveen and Utrecht) showed such conformity that it seemed justified to discuss them together. Table 1 gives the results of the three questionnaires for the two towns separately. Second, the cooperation of parents in the study was great; most parents filled in the questionnaires. An average of 93% responded, and, they all did this voluntarily. Third, it can be concluded that a questionnaire seems to be a useful instrument and increases the efficiency of the screening process used to identify children with developmental problems. Figure 1 shows (in percentages) the number of children in the three age groups who are classified as normal by the parent questionnaire and who would not need to be given the DOS.

Table 1. Comparison results of three questionnaires in Hoogeveen and Utrecht

Questionnaire result (Number of questions answered negatively)	10 months DOS result				1½ years DOS result				2¼ years DOS result			
	Hoogeveen		Utrecht		Hoogeveen		Utrecht		Hoogeveen		Utrecht	
	Normal	Non-normal	Normal	Non-normal	Normal	Non-normal	Normal	Non-normal	Normal	Non-normal	Normal	Non-normal
	N	N	N	N	N	N	N	N	N	N	N	N
0	146	0	33	0	136	0	21	1	157	1	8	0
1	80	0	23	2	164	3	23	4	129	3	17	1
2	45	3	19	1	103	4	15	1	104	1	24	4
3	15	1	12	4	56	7	18	1	52	3	18	3
4 or more	8	2	14	5	61	29	10	12	90	12	36	6
Total	294	6	101	12	520	43	87	19	532	20	103	14

10 months

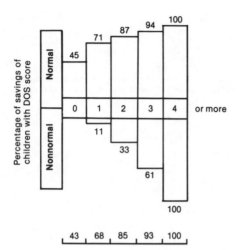

at the criterion of maximum number
of questions answered negatively

Total percentage of savings per
criterion

1½ years

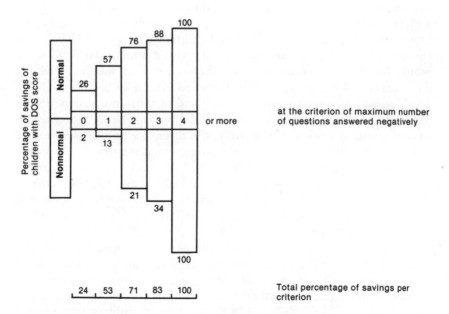

at the criterion of maximum number
of questions answered negatively

Total percentage of savings per
criterion

Figure 1.   Percentage of children not needing DOS evaluation had the questionnaire been
interpreted as normal with scores of 0–4 or more answered "no."

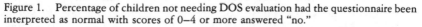

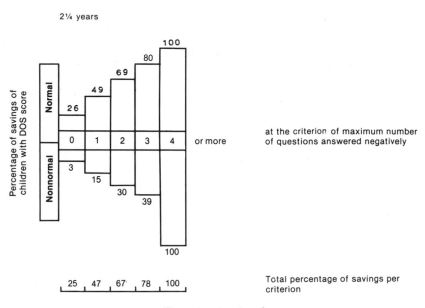

Figure 1.   Continued.

The number of questions answered "no" on the questionnaire was used as the criterion to determine whether the child needed to be tested with the DOS. At the most conservative criterion (no questions answered negatively), 43% of the 10-month-old children would need to be given the questionnaire only, and yet no child with a nonnormal DOS score would be missed. Success for the other age groups was less striking, although certainly it should not be dismissed. About 25% of the children would need to be tested with the DOS and of those not tested, 2% to 3% with nonnormal DOS scores would be missed. Using the criterion of one question answered negatively, the three age groups were rather alike concerning the percentage of children with nonnormal DOS scores that would be missed, respectively, 11%, 13%, and 15%. On the other hand, the savings of not testing with the DOS would be, respectively, 69%, 53%, and 47%. Using the criterion of two questions answered negatively, it seems that at two ages (10 months and 2¼ years) 33% or nearly one-third of the children with nonnormal DOS scores would be missed, but at the age of 1½ years, the percentage would be 20. The savings in the number of children not needing the DOS ranged from 67% to 86%. The criterion of three questions answered negatively yielded a much greater number of missed nonnormal DOS scores, but there was only a small decrease in the number of children who needed to be given the DOS. These considerations concerning savings versus missed children should be seen in the light of the validity of the DOS.

From early findings, it was reported that a screening procedure with only the DOS at the age of 10 months did not prove to be very effective from a screening-technical point of view (Cools and Hermanns, 1977, 1979). It finally seemed that only a small number of children with developmental problems could be detected by the DOS at this age. A questionnaire did not make an additional contribution in detecting developmental problems.

At the age of 1½ years, the DOS proved valid and useful. The test detected a reasonable number of children with developmental problems and the questionnaire enhanced the number of children identified. When the criterion of no-question-answered-negatively was used, about 25% of the children did not need to be tested with the DOS. Calculating 15 minutes to administer the DOS, this implies a savings of 6 test hours per 100 children. This savings proves to be even more impressive at a less conservative criterion. It must be considered, however, that more children and nonnormal DOS scores are missed when the less conservative criterion is used.

It was possible to conduct further analysis on the effectiveness in terms of different criteria for suspect scores on the questionnaires using the 1½-year-old children with nonnormal DOS scores who were tested in the longitudinal study. Of the 43 children with nonnormal DOS scores, 24 were confirmed as having developmental problems on follow-up. Using the criterion of one question answered negatively, none of these 24 children was missed. When the criterion of two questions answered negatively was used, one child was missed. When the criterion of three questions answered negatively was applied, two children were missed. All of those children identified as having developmental problems by low developmental test scores or pediatric evaluations, had questionnaire scores of more than three questions answered negatively. In Hoogeveen, a less conservative criterion would have missed children with nonnormal DOS scores. These children proved, however, to be unjustly indicated as suspect (false positives) or to have a less serious problem than the children who would not have been missed. This criterion might imply a savings of more than 80% in the number of tests that need to be administered.

Concerning the data on the validity of the DOS at the age of 2¼ years, the test also proved rather efficient at this age. Twenty children had nonnormal DOS scores. Of these 20, ten had confirmed developmental problems. Thus, the questionnaire can also make a valuable contribution for screening children at this age. The percentages of savings of time in administering tests to children by the use of the parent questionnaire at 1½ years holds true at 2¼ years as well.

The fourth point to be made in discussing the results is that the questionnaire was considered useful because the parents' responses proved to be reliable generally speaking. Before recommending the use of the questionnaire, however, it seemed necessary to investigate to what extent parents had answered the questions correctly. The method for investigating this was as follows. Because the items on the questionnaire were DOS items reworded as questions, the children were given the DOS by a specially trained tester after the questionnaire had been completed. Thus, it was possible to calculate to what extent the answers to the questions and the scores on the corresponding DOS items agreed.

Table 2 shows the results. The data of Hoogeveen and those of Utrecht show great parallelism. The percentages of agreement on items from the DOS and the 10-months questionnaire range from 84% to 99%. Those for 1½ years range from 81% to 99%, and those for 2¼ years range from 59% to 100%. On the questionnaires for 10 months and 1½ years, it seems that there is little difference in the percentage of agreement with the DOS items when the individual sectors of the test are considered. The relatively lower percentage of agreement for the 2¼-years questionnaire were on items from the adaptive and gross motor sectors of the test and reflect questions, which may have been somewhat more difficult for parents to answer accurately. The items "Draw vertical line" and "Stand on one foot for 1 second" had the lowest agreement. These items concern performances that the children may not have been

Table 2.   Percent of parent responses scored correct by DOS

Questions referring to items from sectors	10 months	1½ years	2¼ years
Personal-social	90	88	86
	98	95	99
		95	100
			100
Fine motor-	84	93	64
adaptive	87	93	68
	93	97	99
Language	90	90	87
	96	93	89
		96	92
			92
			97
Gross motor	95	95	59
	96	97	65
	99	99	96
			98
Mean	93	94	97
Highest value	99	99	100
Lowest value	84	88	59

able to do because of their age, and the questions required the parents to judge the degree of accuracy of the vertical line and the length of time the child balanced on one foot. The differences found were due primarily to the parents giving positive responses versus negative DOS-item scores to these relatively unreliable questions on the 2¼-years questionnaire. In all other cases, there was no question of such a clear tendency.

In summary, the parents were found to give accurate answers to the questions and proved to be good assessors of their child's developmental level with the aid of a questionnaire. In general, they did not give a greater value to their child's performance than proved to be justified in the standardized situation.

CONCLUSION

The questionnaire was found to be a useful instrument for increasing efficiency of the process of early detection of developmental problems. This is said primarily from a screening-technical point of view and on the assumption that the questionnaire will not be used by itself but with the DOS. The fact that the child does not meet any of the specific criterion for the questionnaire does not imply that he or she will have a nonnormal DOS score. The savings that the questionnaire yielded will be lost by further attention to the false positives that it generates if it is not followed by the DOS.

There are other important aspects that play a role in applying the questionnaire. As is mentioned in the beginning of this chapter, attention was drawn to the emotional implications of screening. It is important to consider how the questionnaire should be presented to the parents and how to make them understand that their child need not be able to perform all of the tasks. Another critical consideration follows the application of the questionnaire. Whichever scoring criterion is used for the questionnaire, the decision to apply the DOS should not automatically imply that the child's development is not normal although this seems to be suggested. Making the process from the first administration of the questionnaire and following it with the DOS run smoothly requires a skill that can only be mentioned in this report. During the training received by the research project assistants, how not to alarm or upset parents or falsely label their child was discussed at length. The results of this research made it possible to include the questionnaire in the third edition of the DOS manual so that application of the questionnaire and administration of the DOS can be integrated.

After the DOS, the parents were interviewed by a psychological assistant using questions that had been previously formulated. The object was to gain insight into the child's environment and the parent-child interaction.

It can be stated that the interview did not add to the accuracy of screening with the DOS. The reason for this could not be determined on the basis of the data. A side-effect of the interview that can be considered as beneficial should be noted. Although the parents did not necessarily volunteer additional information to the interviewer, they seemed motivated to ask for additional information about their children because of the interview.

The observation provided some benefit. The absence of "Positive reinforcement" in combination with the presence of "Negative reinforcement" showed connection with developmental problems; thus, parents' responsiveness to their children proved to be possibly indicative. In this way, these observation variables can contribute to the process of early detection. In practical terms, however, this is hard to realize. In the first place, very intensive training is needed before one can observe well; moreover, it does not seem possible when large numbers of children are involved. In this particular research, the observation was done by a special assistant. In conclusion, it seems difficult to determine finer methods that might increase the accuracy of the process of early detection.

REFERENCES

Cools, A. T. M., and Hermanns, J. M. A. 1977. Vroegtijdige onderkenning van problemen in de ontwikkeling van kinderen; constructie en toepassing van de Denver Ontwikkeling Screeningtest. (Early diagnosis of problems in the development of children: construction and application of the Denver Developmental Screening Test) Amsterdam, Swets en Zeitlinger.

Cools, A. T. M., and Hermanns, J. M. A. 1979. (Denver Developmental Screening Test: Manual) Denver Ontwikkeling Screeningtest; handleiding. Amsterdam, Swets en Zeitlinger, 3e herziene druk.

Frankenburg, W. K., van Doorninck, W. J., Liddell, T. N., and Dick, N. P. 1976. The Denver Prescreening Developmental Questionnaire (PDQ). *Pediatrics* 57:744–753.

Frankenburg, W. K. (Ed.), Proceedings of the Second International Conference on Developmental Screening. University of Colorado Medicine Center Press, Denver, CO.

Riksen-Walraven, J. M. A. 1977. Stimulation of early child development: an intervention experiment. Stimulering van de vroeg-kinderlijke ontwikkeling; een interventie-experiment. Amsterdam, Swets en Zeitlinger.

Chapter 10
Early Screening Inventory:
A Study of Early Childhood Developmental Screening

Martha Stone Wiske, Samuel J. Meisels, Terrence Tivnan

Developmental screening instruments are widely administered to infants and young children as a way of identifying those individuals who may need further evaluation and special educational assistance (Cross and Goin, 1977; Gallagher and Bradley, 1972; Meisels, 1978). In recent years screening instruments have proliferated in response to increased interest in the early detection and remediation of handicaps. Unfortunately, insufficient attention has been given to the systematic construction, validation, and interpretation of these instruments.

This chapter describes the process of constructing the Early Screening Inventory (ESI) (Meisels and Wiske, 1976, in press) and reports on studies undertaken to assess its effectiveness in identifying children with potential educational handicaps.[1] The ESI is administered to children from 4 to 6 years old to identify individuals for whom early educational intervention may prevent or ameliorate later school failure.

The intent of this chapter is to examine some of the dilemmas encountered in developing, validating, and interpreting screening instruments and to describe one approach to these problems. The first section clarifies the purpose of the ESI and presents data regarding its construction and composition. Next, the results of two reliability studies performed on the ESI are given. The third section focuses on validity.

---

[1] The ESI was formerly known as the Eliot-Pearson Screening Inventory (EPSI). It is now called the Early Screening Inventory (Meisels and Wiske, in press).

Both concurrent and predictive validity data are presented and discussed. The conclusion addresses issues of the utility of screening instruments and discusses the interpretation of ESI results within the context of a comprehensive early intervention effort.

THE DEVELOPMENT OF THE EARLY SCREENING INVENTORY

Description and Purpose

The ESI is a 15-minute developmental survey administered individually to children 4 to 6 years of age. Through a brief assessment of perceptual, motor, and language functioning, the ESI is designed to identify those children who may need special educational services in order to perform adequately in school. The ESI is only one part of a total screening program that includes a parent questionnaire, a medical examination, and vision and hearing tests.

The ESI is not a diagnostic instrument. The primary purpose of the ESI is to distinguish quickly and efficiently children whose developmental abilities are at least average for their age from children whose developmental abilities seem delayed. Its design reflects an assumption that young children with delayed development are at risk for later school failure. Once this at-risk group is identified by the ESI, further evaluation of each child is necessary to determine if in fact a developmental problem does exist, what the problem is, and what type of educational intervention will best serve the child's needs.

Content

The ESI is divided into three main sections: Visual-Motor/Adaptive, Language and Cognition, and Gross Motor/Body Awareness. The Visual-Motor/Adaptive section examines fine motor control, eye-hand coordination, the ability to remember visual sequence, the ability to draw visual forms (two dimensional), and the ability to reproduce visual structures (three dimensional). The Language and Cognition items examine language comprehension and verbal expression, the ability to reason and count, and the ability to remember auditory sequences. The Gross Motor/Body Awareness section examines balance, large motor coordination, and the ability to imitate body positions from visual cues. In addition to these three sections, the ESI includes two additional items: The Draw-A-Person task (DAP) and letter writing.

Although each section was designed to investigate a child's ability within a particular area, no section is meant to stand alone. A child's relative strengths and weaknesses across sections can and should be noted, but they must be regarded only as general trends. Any conclusions drawn from ESI results are based on the overall performance.

Preliminary Development of the ESI[2]

All of the ESI items were selected or adapted from well-known and widely used developmental instruments. Items were selected that could be reliably administered and scored and that covered the range of relevant abilities within the three developmental areas. Although several items are more closely associated with school readiness (e.g., color naming, counting) than with ability to learn, they were included because they are well normed items and can indicate whether a child has learned what the majority of children his or her age have learned. Finally, the ESI was designed to use a small number of inexpensive and easily obtainable materials that appeal to young children.

Based on trial-testing with more than 3,000 children and preliminary reliability and validity studies, the ESI underwent four major revisions. These early studies are described by Schlossberg (1978). Schlossberg's work led to revision and modification of ESI items and to a refinement of scoring and interpretation guidelines. Based on her findings, a child's total ESI score is interpreted according to the following guidelines (calculated separately for 4- and 5-year-old children):

Refer—total score lower than two standard deviations below the mean
Rescreen—total score between one and two standard deviations below the mean
OK—total score higher than one standard deviation below the mean

Subjects with scores in the Rescreen range receive another screening administration in 8 to 10 weeks, at which time a decision regarding referral for evaluation is made.

The item analysis, reliability, and validity studies reported in this chapter were conducted on the fourth version of the ESI (Meisels and Wiske, 1976, in press). This version incorporates the revisions suggested by Schlossberg.

Item Analysis

An analysis was performed to determine if each item on the ESI discriminates between children who pass the screening with no apparent difficulty and children who are referred for further evaluation. A sample of 465 children ages 4 years 2 months to 5 years 10 months was randomly selected from public preschool and elementary school programs in a predominantly working and lower middle class urban community with a mean income of $10,265 as reported in 1970. All of the children were

---

[2] Portions of this section were adapted from B. Schlossberg *The Development of a Developmental Screening Test for Young Children* (unpublished master's thesis, Tufts University, 1978).

Caucasian and English-speaking. Of the 465 children whose ESI results were recorded, 24 children were referred for further evaluation (Refer group), and 441 children passed the screening process (OK and Rescreen group).

The percentage of children who passed each item was recorded for both groups. The results indicated that the ESI items clearly discriminate between the OK and the Refer groups. Only the components of items— copy forms and verbal reasoning—did not clearly discriminate between the OK and Refer groups. These components, however, are arranged in order of increasing difficulty, and nearly all children passed the easiest components.

When the items are examined as a whole, they do discriminate between the two groups. With only one exception (the Skip item), at least 75% of the OK Subjects passed each item, and approximately 60% of the Refer Subjects failed each item. Thus, distinct performance differentiation between the two groups is obtainable from an analysis of individual items.

RELIABILITY AND MEASUREMENT ERROR OF THE ESI

Two potential sources of error were evaluated as part of the reliability studies performed on the ESI: 1) inconsistencies in test administration and scoring, and 2) inconsistency or instability in responses of the subject over time.

Interscorer Reliability

A tester-observer procedure was utilized to measure the degree of variation in scoring. The tester and observer each scored the same performance, rendering two sets of scores for each test performance. A total of three examiners and 18 Subjects were included in this study. Ten of the Subjects were males and eight were females; 11 of them were 4 years old and seven were age 5. The subjects were chosen randomly from several different preschool classrooms. The roles of tester and observer were alternated for control purposes.

Correlations were obtained between the testers and the observers for the three subdivisions of the ESI and for the ESI total score. All of the interscorer reliability coefficients were higher than 0.80; the total score correlation was 0.91. Although these findings are based on a small number of subjects and raters, when reviewed in conjunction with the test-retest results, they indicate high reliability for the ESI as a whole.

Test-Retest Reliability

The test-retest reliability study was designed to examine both interrater reliability and test stability over time. The study design called for two examiners to administer the ESI to the same subject on two occasions, approximately 1 week apart. A measure of error variance due to changes in the testing environment, the general disposition of the subject, or other similar factors was obtained.

A total of six examiners and 57 Subjects were involved in this study. The Subjects included 28 males and 29 females, ages 4 years to 5 years 10 months, who were randomly selected from several preschool and kindergarten classrooms. The roles of test examiner and retest examiner were varied for control purposes. The correlation for the total score on the ESI test-retest administrations was 0.82. This coefficient indicates the stability of measurement of equivalent scores based on identical forms of the ESI administered 7 to 10 days apart, without intervening practice or direct instruction.

Although correlations for all three subscales are below 0.80, the key statistic is the correlation for the total ESI score, which is 0.82. The subsequent analyses (discussed in this chapter) make use primarily of the total score. In practical application, only the total score of the ESI should be used for decisions regarding the need for further evaluation.

THE VALIDITY OF THE ESI

Validity is a measure of an instrument's effectiveness in accomplishing what it purports to do. As screening instruments have proliferated, controversy has developed concerning the appropriate methodology for establishing their validity. The major issues involve identifying appropriate criterion measures and determining the most informative means of comparing such measures with screening results. Because these matters are controversial, a brief explanation of the rational for the design of the present studies is presented.

Debate concerning the selection of a criterion is tied to questions about the purpose of screening. In the past, comprehensive evaluations of development or intelligence were often used as the criterion against which developmental screening tests were validated (Frankenburg, Camp, and Van Natta, 1971). Such comparisons are intended to establish that the screening instrument under investigation is a valid indicator of current development. To the degree that intelligence tests are correlated with later school success, such studies may also establish a screening instrument's predictive validity. If the purpose of screening, however, is to identify children who may need assistance in order to succeed in school, then additional appropriate criteria for validation are longitudinal data reflecting actual school performance. Several recent studies of developmental screening instruments have used longitudinal school data, such as achievement or readiness test scores, teacher ratings of student performance, or participation in remedial reading classes as a criterion

(Barnes, 1978; Feshbach, Adelman, and Fuller, 1974; Mardell and Goldenberg, 1978; Satz and Friel, 1979; Schaefer, 1978). On the assumption that screening tests should both detect developmental delays and identify children who may encounter school difficulty, the ESI validation studies utilize both concurrent and longitudinal criterion measures. These measures include concurrent scores on the *McCarthy Scales of Children's Ability* (McCarthy, 1972) and several measures of academic performance in kindergarten through fourth grade.

In longitudinal studies, such as the one reported here, treatment becomes a confounding variable. In theory, children who do poorly on screening should receive intervention services. These services are expected to improve school performance and thereby to decrease the predictive accuracy of the screening results. None of the children in this study received special intervention services during the kindergarten year. Any subsequent special educational assistance was not controlled for in this study. Thus, any special treatment supplied to children after kindergarten may have reduced the predictive accuracy of positive screening results. Presumably, the predictive accuracy of negative screening results should not have been affected by this treatment.

Another major issue regarding validation studies is the selection of an appropriate statistic or design for comparing screening and outcome results. Correlation coefficients are frequently used to indicate overall relationships between screening and criterion test results. Additional analyses must be performed, however, to determine how frequently individual children are incorrectly identified during the screening process. Several researchers have recommended using contingency tables to clarify the frequency and nature of misclasssifications made during the screening process (Frankenburg and Camp, 1975; Mercer, Algozzine, and Trifiletti, 1979; Satz and Fletcher, 1979). In this study both correlation coefficients and contingency tables are presented in order to clarify the relationship between the ESI and criterion results.

Concurrent Validity

This study was designed to analyze the accuracy of ESI results as a measure of current developmental level. The criterion measure selected for this investigation was the McCarthy Scales of Children's Abilities (MSCA) (McCarthy, 1972), a widely used comprehensive developmental evaluation instrument.

The MSCA is designed to assess the developmental level of children from 2½ to 8½ years of age. It consists of 18 subtests of mental and motor ability, which are grouped into five indices. A sixth index, the General Cognitive Index (GCI), is an overall score derived from the verbal, perceptual performance, and quantitative indices. The McCarthy is a standardized norm-referenced test. For the GCI there is a mean score of 100 and a standard deviation of 16. The reliability coefficients for the CGI average 0.93. Validity information on the McCarthy is limited (Kaufman and Kaufman, 1977).

Method   A stratified sample of 102 Subjects was selected from six different school systems in the metropolitan Boston area. Nearly all Subjects were Caucasian (a few were black and Oriental), and all were English-speaking. The ESI was administered by experienced and trained screeners to all age-appropriate children in three of these school systems, and to a small sample of children likely to be referred for evaluation in the remaining school systems. As children were identified who fulfilled the criteria established for the study sample, they were assigned to an experienced evaluator for administration of the MSCA. The MSCA was administered 7 to 10 days after initial screening.

Sample   Table 1 shows the characteristics of the 102 children who participated in this study. The sample was stratified in terms of age, sex, socioeconomic status (SES), and results on the ESI (i.e., OK, or Refer for further evaluation). The sample was selected to include nearly equal numbers of boys and girls and of 4- and 5-year-olds, as well as closely comparable distributions of children in terms of SES and results on the ESI. The definitions of occupational groupings were condensed from the format used for the MSCA (McCarthy, 1972). Every attempt was made to have a representation of each specific occupation in these two SES groupings (see Table 1).

Similarly, every effort was made to obtain a large representation of Refer Subjects. Thus, in the design of this study, the OK/Refer populations were obtained by collapsing the continuous distribution of ESI scores into two categories, and by including in the sample a large number of Subjects with scores in the Refer group. By including a larger number of subjects who scored in the lower range on the ESI, a more comprehensive analysis of the ESI's accuracy in identifying children at risk could be performed.

Results   Several different analyses were performed with the data from this study. A correlation coefficient of 0.73 was obtained from comparison of the ESI total score with the GCI. Further analyses indicate that this correlation remains unchanged by the effects on the sample of age, sex, or SES. Thus it can be inferred from these data that the ESI generally measures the same domain of skills, knowledge, and abilities that are measured by the GCI of the MSCA.

In order to increase the practical significance of the comparison of results on both instruments, subjects were divided according to their scoring category on the ESI (i.e., OK, Rescreen, or Refer). The cutoffs that define these categories—one and two standard deviations below the

Table 1.   Characteristics of concurrent validity sample

Characteristic	Number of subjects
Age	
4 years 2 months–4 years 11 months	51
5 years–5 years 11 months	51
Sex	
male	52
female	50
SES[a]	
low	56
mid–high	46
ESI results	
refer	37
OK	65

[a] Two occupational groupings were specified for this standardization study. The categories represent a condensation of the five groups used for the standardization of the MSCA. The two groups are

Occupational group	Nature of occupation
Low	Laborers; unskilled workers; operatives; service workers and semiskilled workers
Mid-high	Craftsmen and foremen (skilled workers); managers, officials, and proprietors; clerical workers; sales workers; professional and technical workers

mean—were also used to divide subjects on the basis of their McCarthy GCI score. A comparison of performances on the two instruments, using these scoring categories, is presented in Table 2.

The implications of Table 2 can best be understood if it is considered how the ESI results could be used in actual practice. In common practice, the 12 children shown in Table 2 as scoring in the Rescreen range on the ESI would receive a second screening within 2 months. On the basis of this screening each child would be assigned to either the OK or the Refer group. Assuming that the children whose original ESI scores placed them in cells d and e would eventually be assigned to the Refer groups, and that those in cell f would be placed in the OK group, another comparison of the two instruments can be made (see Table 3). Table 3 illustrates that a strong relationship exists between the ESI and MSCA.

Short-Term Predictive Validity

Additional analyses were undertaken to determine how accurately the ESI predicts the level of academic readiness achieved by children at the

Table 2.   Comparisons of performances on ESI and
MSCA ($N = 102$)

ESI/MSCA	GCI = <68*	GCI = 68–84**	GCI = >84***
Refer*	8[a]	9[b]	8[c]
Rescreen**	2[d]	1[e]	9[f]
OK***	0[g]	3[h]	62[i]

* indicates a score less than two standard deviations below the mean.

** indicates a score between one and two standard deviations below the mean.

*** indicates a score within one standard deviation of the mean or higher.

end of their kindergarten year. For this study, ESI scores obtained prior to or in the first 2 months of the kindergarten year were correlated with a readiness test given at the end of kindergarten. The *Metropolitan Readiness Test* (MRT) was used as the criterion measure.

The MRT is a norm-referenced, multiple choice, group- administered test that is designed to predict readiness for first-grade instruction. Revised in 1976 (Nurss and McGauvran, 1976), it consists of two levels and two forms for each level. The MRT was normed with more than 100,000 kindergarten and first-grade children. Split-half reliability estimates for the MRT prereading skills composite score are at the 0.90 level. Predictive validity for the MRT was obtained by correlating scores obtained on the MRT in the fall with achievement scores obtained in the spring from the Metropolitan Achievement Test. Substantial validity correlations (0.70 with both total reading and total math achievement scores) were obtained for both levels of the MRT (Nurss and McGauvran, 1976).

Method   The sample included all children tested with the MRT at the end of their kindergarten year who had been previously screened with the ESI ($N = 472$). The sample was drawn from the same community where the reliability study took place. It was stratified by age (42% ages 4 years, 3 months to 4 years 11 months, and 58% ages 5 years to 5 years 11 months) and by sex (49% females and 51% males).

Table 3.   Comparisons of performances on
ESI and MSCA ($N = 102$)

ESI	MSCA Refer	MSCA OK
Refer	20[a,b,d,e]	8[c]
OK	3[g,h]	71[f,i]

Note: Superscripts refer to Table 2.

The length of time that elapsed between the administrations of the ESI and the MRT ranged from 7 months to 1 year. The ESI was administered by experienced teachers of young children who were trained and supervised by one of the authors. The MRT (Form P, Level II) was administered by kindergarten teachers to their own students as a part of the regular school program. The MRT prereading skills composite score, expressed as a percentile based on local norms for kindergarten children, was used as the criterion variable.

Results   Correlation coefficients between ESI total scores and the MRT local percentiles were obtained. These correlations are substantially unchanged when the sample of children is analyzed by age or by sex. The correlation coefficients show a moderate relationship between the ESI and the MRT scores that is highly statistically significant (4-year-olds = 0.44; 5-year-olds = 0.49; males = 0.45; females = 0.46; total = 0.45; $p < 0.001$).

The relationship between the two instruments is further clarified by means of a contingency table analysis. Subjects were divided into four groups based on their EST and MRT scores. They were assigned to the Low group on the ESI if their total ESI score was at or below the 15th percentile for their age group. The population was further divided according to their MRT scores, again using the 15 percentile as the cutoff. The 15th percentile was selected as the cutoff point for this comparison because it corresponds to a reasonable proportion of children to be recognized as needing further attention based on screening results. In a normally distributed sample, this cutoff point corresponds to a score approximately one standard deviation below the mean. Table 4 shows the crosstabulation of the ESI and MRT results.

Cell *a* in Table 4 shows the number of children whose scores fell below the 15th percentile on both tests; cell *d* shows the children whose scores were above this cutoff on both tests. Together, cells *a* and *b* indicate the number of children who were correctly classified on the basis of screening, using the MRT as a criterion. When expressed as a percentage of the total sample, this figure, (83%), is an indication of the overall agreement between the two tests. Cell *c* in Table 4 shows that 44 children scored high on the screening but low on the criterion test.

Table 4.   Crosstabulation of ESI totals and MRT local percentiles ($N = 472$)

	MRT percentile	
ESI percentile	Low (≤ 15th)	High (> 15th)
Low (≤ 15th)	22[a]	38[b]
High (> 15th)	44[c]	369[d]

This number represents 9% of the total sample and 67% of the children who scored low on the MRT. Cell *b* shows the number of children who scored poorly on screening but did well on the MRT. The 38 children in this category accounted for 8% of the total sample, or 9% of those children who scored high on the MRT.

The high percent agreement (83%) between these two tests indicates that ESI results are a good predictor of reading readiness at the end of kindergarten. The agreement is not perfect, as might be expected, in part because the ESI covers a wide range of development than reading-related abilities alone.

Longitudinal Predictive Validity

A further study tested the accuracy of ESI scores in predicting later school success. The study was also designed so that ESI results could be compared with the results of other screening procedures in terms of their accuracy in predicting later school performance. The ESI is administered in conjunction with other screening procedures—medical, vision, and hearing testing as well as a parent questionnaire concerned with the child's developmental and medical background. Data from this study were collected and analyzed in order to determine whether developmental screening added to the predictive accuracy of the other elements of the screening process.

For this analysis, indicators of the subjects' actual school performance in kindergarten through fourth grade were used as the outcome measures. Data from school records formed the basis for three criterion variables: 1) a *cumulative score* derived from report-card grades in reading, math, and spelling; 2) indication of whether the child received or was referred for *special educational services*; and 3) *disposition* at the end of the school year (promoted or retained in grade).

Method   The sample included 115 children enrolled in public kindergarten through fourth grade who had participated in the screening program prior to or just after entering kindergarten. The SES, race, and ethnic backgrounds of this sample were identical to those of the reliability study. The children were randomly selected from classrooms in two elementary schools whose teachers volunteered to cooperate with the study. Only children who had received a complete screening battery were included in the study. From this sample, 20 to 28 students were randomly selected from each grade. Correlation and multiple stepwise regression analyses were performed to determine the predictive power of the ESI and to compare it with the predictive accuracy of other screening results.

Results   The results are presented in Table 5. The three columns of Table 5 report correlations between school outcomes, and respec-

Table 5.   Regression analysis of screening results and later school performance

Criterion variable	N	Correlation coefficients for total ESI score	Multiple R for parent questionnaire, vision, hearing, and medical screening only	Multiple R for ESI added to other screening variables
Kindergarten				
Cumulative score	46	0.70***	0.61	0.79**
Special services	(none available)			
Disposition	34	0.47	0.61	0.74
First grade				
Cumulative score	69	0.50***	0.41	0.65**
Special services	69	0.42**	0.33	0.54**
Disposition	42	0.30	0.41	0.48
Second grade				
Cumulative score	53	0.52***	0.39	0.66**
Special services	53	0.51**	0.36	0.62*
Disposition	35	0.57***	0.60	0.77**
Third grade				
Cumulative score	36	0.31*	0.38	0.48
Special services	36	0.53**	0.57	0.70
Disposition	(no variation)			
Fourth grade				
Cumulative score	21	0.33	0.55	0.63
Special services	21	0.41*	0.66	0.67
Disposition	(no variation)			

* $p < 0.05$.

** $p < 0.01$.

*** $p < 0.001$.

Note: All available data about school performance were recorded for each subject. Information from previous grades was available only for some subjects. Consequently, the correlation between screening results and, for example, first grade performance is based on a larger number of subjects than just those subjects enrolled in first grade at the time of the study.

tively, the ESI scores alone, all other screening results (parent questionnaire, vision, hearing, medical), and the ESI scores combined with the other screening results.

It can be seen in Table 5 that ESI results are significantly correlated with at least some measures of performance from kindergarten through fourth grade. These correlations are highest and most significant between ESI scores and report-card grades in kindergarten through second grade. A significant correlation is also found between the ESI results and the need for special education services in third and fourth grade.

The last two columns of Table 5 demonstrate the predictive strength that the ESI adds to other screening results. In every case, the regression coefficient between screening results and later school performance is increased when the ESI scores are added to the results of the other screening components. For several measures of performance in kindergarten through second grade, the inclusion of ESI results in the regression calculation made the regression coefficient statistically significant. In no case was the coefficient significant between the other screening results (without the ESI) and the measures of school performance.

As a way of supplementing the information on predictive validity, contingency table analyses were performed. Subjects were divided into four categories based on screening and criterion results using the 15th percentile as a cutoff. Table 6 summarizes the results of the analyses.

The first column in Table 6 shows the number of students for whom the appropriate information was available. The next two columns indicate the percentages of children who were correctly classified by the ESI, using the 15th percentile as the cutoff score for both the ESI and the criterion variable. The overall percent agreement between the ESI and each of the measures of school performance can be obtained by combining these two percentages. The last two columns of Table 6 present the percentages of children who were not correctly classified by the ESI. Children may be incorrectly classified either because they scored above the 15th percentile on the ESI and subsequently had problems in school, or because they scored at or below the 15th percentile on the ESI but showed no major problems on the outcome measures selected for analysis. These two types of incorrect classification are frequently referred to as false negatives and false positives, respectively.

The results shown in Table 6 indicate that the overall agreement between the ESI and the various criterion measures is fairly high. The total percentage of correctly classified children ranges from 64% to 79%; moreover, there is relatively little variation from kindergarten through fourth grade. The columns displaying the incorrect classifications show that the false negative rate is consistently lower than the false positive rate.

Table 6.   Crosstabulations of ESI scores and later school performance

		Correctly classified		Incorrectly classified	
Criterion variable	N	% OK on ESI and outcome	% low on ESI and outcome	% high on ESI, low on outcome	% low on ESI, high on outcome
Kindergarten					
Cumulative score	53	70	13	2	15
Special services (none provided in Kindergarten)					
Disposition	38	55	24	0	21
First grade					
Cumulative score	78	60	15	1	23
Special services	85	59	15	4	22
Disposition	48	48	21	8	23
Second grade					
Cumulative score	60	58	13	0	28
Special services	62	52	21	5	23
Disposition	41	51	22	2	24
Third grade					
Cumulative score	42	48	17	5	31
Special services	42	52	26	0	21
Disposition	(no variation)				
Fourth grade					
Cumulative score	23	61	9	9	22
Special services	23	65	9	4	22
Disposition	(not available)				

Two considerations are worth noting in the analysis of false negative and false positive rates. First, the availability of special services generally tends to increase the rate of false positives by improving the subsequent school performance of children who score low on screening tests. Second, false positive and false negative rates are influenced by the selection of cutoff points on the screening test and on the criterion measures. In general, as the false positive or overreferral rate is decreased, the false negative or underreferral rate increases, and vice versa.

In summary, both the results from the regression analyses and the results from the contingency table analyses indicate that the ESI makes a substantial contribution to prediction of later school performance. When utilized as one element of an early intervention program, the ESI can serve as a valuable tool for identifying children who may require special educational services.

SUMMARY AND DISCUSSION

Based on the evidence presented in this chapter, it can be concluded that the ESI is a valid and reliable screening instrument. It was developed in order to identify those children who might require special educational intervention in order to succeed in school. The results of concurrent, short-term, and longitudinal predictive validity studies indicate that, in general, the ESI is a good predictor of current development and of future school performance.

However, the validity and reliability of a screening instrument are not the only issues to be considered in assessing the value of a screening program. Test validity and the ethics of assessment are not identical (Messick, 1980). That is, the identification of young children at risk for school failure is useful only if something can be done to help these children. Thus, a screening instrument must be interpreted within the context of the resources and services available for assessing and meeting the needs of children referred through the screening process.

This point can be illustrated by looking more closely at the issue of false positives and false negatives. As noted above, the proportion of false inclusions and false exclusions is dependent on the selection of a cutoff score for the screening instrument. If the cutoff score is raised, more children are referred for evaluation and the proportion of false negatives increases; if it is lowered, fewer children are referred and the false negative rate increases. Setting the cutoff point is a matter of judgment. There is no absolute or clear standard for its selection.

In determining the cutoff point for referrals, the users of a screening instrument must weigh the consequences of misclassification. Is it better to identify falsely a normal child as at risk or to overlook falsely a child with special needs? The answer must take into account such issues as the potential consequences on the child and family of labeling, the detrimental effects of postponing needed intervention, the availability of diagnostic services, and the quality and quantity of intervention programs. Local norms should thus be established within the context of community needs and resources.

There is another perspective on the screening context that offers the potential for reducing both false positives and false negatives. Additional information should be gathered about a child to supplement the screening results before making a final decision about the need for referral. Parents, teachers, and the data obtainable from other components in the screening process are important sources of such information. Teachers trained in diagnostic-prescriptive techniques can provide informal educational assessments and individually designed programming for children. Combined with these services, screening can become a first step in responsive teaching rather than simply a first step in the special education evaluation process.

In short, screening instruments and their attributes of validity and predictability must be viewed as components of a much larger educational system. No screening instrument can be accurately assessed without this comprehensive perspective on the child and the community.

ACKNOWLEDGMENTS

We gratefully acknowledge the assistance we received from the teachers and school administrators who cooperated with us in our preparation of this study. We also thank Ms. Beth Schlossberg for her early work on the development of the ESI, and Drs. Marc Lieberman and Anthony Bryk for their methodological consultation.

REFERENCES

Barnes, E. 1978. The Jansky predictive index: A cross-validation study. In: W. K. Frankenburg (ed.), Proceedings of the Second International Conference on Developmental Screening, pp. 23–45. JFK Child Development Center, University of Colorado, Denver.

Cross, L., and Goin, K. (eds.). 1977. Identifying Handicapped Children: A Guide to Casefinding, Screening, Diagnosis, Assessment, and Evaluation. Walker and Company, New York.

Feshbach, S., Adelman, H., and Fuller, W. W. 1974. Early identification of children with high risk of reading failure. J. Learn. Disabil. 7, 639–644.

Frankenburg, W. K., Camp, B. W., and Van Natta, P. A. 1971. Validity of the Denver Developmental Screening Test. Child Dev. 42, 475–488.

Frankenburg, W. K., and Camp, B. W. (eds.). 1975. Pediatric Screening Tests. Charles C Thomas, Springfield, IL.

Gallagher, J. J., and Bradley, R. H. 1972. Early identification of developmental difficulties. In: I. J. Gordon (ed.) Early Childhood Education: The Seventy-first Yearbook of the National Society for the Study of Education. University of Chicago Press, Chicago.

Kaufman, A. S., and Kaufman, N. J. 1977. Research on McCarthy Scales and its implications for assessment. J. Learn. Disabil. 10(5), 284–291.

Mardell, C. D., and Goldenberg, D. S. 1978. DIAL as a screening tool. In: W. K. Frankenburg (ed.), Proceedings of the Second International Conference on Developmental Screening, pp. 9–20. JFK Child Development Center, University of Colorado, Denver.

McCarthy, D. 1972. Manual for the McCarthy Scales of Children's Abilities. Psychological Corporation, New York.

Meisels, S. J. 1978. Developmental Screening in Early Childhood: A Guide. National Association for the Education of Young Children, Washington, D.C.

Meisels, S. J., and Wiske, M. S. 1976. The Eliot-Pearson Screening Inventory. Tufts University, Medford, MA.

Meisels, S. J., and Wiske, M. S. The Early Screening Inventory, Teachers College Press, New York. In press.

Mercer, C. S., Algozzine, B., and Trifiletti, J. J. 1979. Early identification: Issues and considerations. Except. Child. 46, 52–54.

Messick, S. 1980. Test validity and the ethics of assessment. Am. Psychol. 35, 11, 1012–1027.

Nurss, J. R., and McGauvran, M. E. 1976. Metropolitan Readiness Tests, Teacher's Manual. Harcourt Brace Jovanovich, New York.

Satz, P., and Fletcher, M. J. 1979. Early Screening Tests: Some Uses and Abuses. J. Learn. Disabil. 12, 65–69.

Satz, P., and Friel, J. 1979. Predictive validity of an abbreviated screening battery. J. Learn. Disabil. 12, 20–24.

Schaefer, E. S. 1978. Parent interview predictors of teacher ratings of school adaptation: Concepts, methods and findings. In: W. K. Frankenburg (ed.), Proceedings of the Second International Conference on Developmental Screening, pp. 243–258. JFK Child Development Center, University of Colorado, Denver.

Schlossberg, B. 1978. The development of a developmental screening test. Unpublished master's thesis. Tufts University, Medford, MA.

Section III

Section III

COMPREHENSIVE IDENTIFICATION PROGRAMS

Chapter 11

From Four to Ten:

An Overall Evaluation of the General Health Screening of Four-Year-Olds

Claes Sundelin, Tore Mellbin,
Jean-Claude Vuille

To understand the problems associated with the evaluation of the general-health screening of 4-year-olds in Sweden, it is necessary to be familiar with some basic facts about the child-health system in Sweden. Preventive child-care in the form of a network of Child Health Centers (CHC) has been in operation in Sweden for more than 40 years. Each CHC is responsible for the supervision of about 200–900 children within a geographically-defined district. A nurse with special training in public- or child-health care is employed in each district. The physician, who examines the children at special clinics 2 to 4 hours per week, is either a pediatric specialist, a physician undergoing pediatric training, or a district medical officer. Pediatricians serve roughly half of the population of children.

In the early 1960s the Swedish National Board of Health and Welfare, as well as many pediatricians, became increasingly concerned about the participation rates for the check-ups at CHCs. Over 99% of all children under one year of age were receiving all of their required evaluations, and over 90% of all children in the second year of life were receiving theirs. Then, however, there was a decrease in participation, so that by 4 years of age only 56% were receiving their preventive health check-ups. It was felt that the preschool preventive health service had to be strengthened so that more disabling conditions could be detected and treated earlier. At the same time, the Central Committee of Handicap Voluntary Organizations in Sweden went to the Minister of Social Affairs, recommending that a special nationwide health screening of all preschool children be established. In 1967 the Minister of Social Affairs assigned to the National Board of Health and Welfare the task of developing regulations for a general health screening of 4-year-olds. After an investigation period and some pilot projects, the nationwide screening program was started in 1968.

In Uppsala as in most of the 23 counties in Sweden, the health screening was incorporated into the existing system of Child Health Care and carried out by the ordinary staff of the CHC. The program was initiated in January 1969, and since January 1971, all 4-year-olds residing in the county have had the possibility of undergoing the check-up. According to the proposals by the National Board of Health and Welfare, the program was composed of the items shown in Table 1.

Children with previously unknown health problems were referred to different specialists at the University Hospital for clinical examination and possible treatment. The ultimate goal of the program was to bring about an improvement of the health status of children, through early detection and treatment of those pathologic conditions and developmental anomalies that are amenable to treatment.

In the early seventies some partial aspects of the effectiveness were analyzed. It was found that the program was feasible with respect to systematic examination and data collection, acceptance by the public and the staff, and with respect to the strain on existing resources. The participation rate was about 98%. Table 2 shows the effectiveness in detecting functionally important health problems with the help of the screening program.

A functionally-important health problem is defined as a disorder that is likely to have a significant and prolonged impact on the child's health and development or to hamper full exploitation of the environment either at present or in the future. On the basis of this concept of a functionally important health problem, the screening in the county of Uppsala showed that 24.7% of all screened children were found to have health deviations. Out of these, 14.7% were newly discovered by the screening. Furthermore, a separate analysis has demonstrated substantial differences between physicians in the rates of correct and unnecessary referrals. Only a small part of these differences could be attributed to professional status or specific experience with the program. They consisted essentially in varying thresholds for what was perceived as a health problem needing treatment.

In an earlier study, Nilsson, Sundelin, and Vuille (1976) a special analysis of the effectiveness of the psychological examination program

Table 1. The screening program

Source of information/ examination	Performed by	Comment
Questionnaire	Parents	Replacing conventional pediatric history. Contains a few very simple questions about the child's mental and emotional development.
Interview concerning child's behavior and development	Nurse	
Assessment of mental development	Nurse/ physician	Draw a man, count 3 objects, participation at examination, observed behavior.
Test of speech development	Nurse/ physician Auxiliary	1969–1970. Simple observation (conversation). Since 1971, specific test: Pronunciation of 10 key words (pictures).
Hearing test	Auxiliary	Audiogram at 250, 500, 1000, 2000, 4000, and 8000 c/s. Pass level = 25 dB.
Vision test	Nurse/ auxiliary	Single symbol. Snellen's E or Bostrom's hook. Each eye tested separately.
Test for bacteriuria	Auxiliary	Uriglox
Height and weight	Auxiliary	
Physical examination	Physician	Special emphasis on motor coordination: 11 items in 1969–1970. Three items since 1971.
Dental examination	Dentist	Orthodontic abnormalities. Caries. Oral hygiene and gingival disease.

Table 2. Newly detected, previously known, and total prevalence of health problems (Rates per 100 children)

Problems	Newly discovered	Previously known	Total
Visual	4.3	2.5	6.8
Auditory	1.3	0.3	1.6
Neurological	0.1	0.6	0.7
Physical	4.5	5.4	9.9
Mental	0.4	0.4	0.8
Emotional	2.6	0.5	3.1
Speech	1.5	0.3	1.8
Total	14.7	10.0	24.7

was based on clinical assessment of referred cases and on data on children who were not referred but nevertheless were seen by a child psychiatrist within 2½ years after the health screening. The purpose of the study was to determine specificity and sensitivity of the instruments to be used in the study described below. The sensitivity of the psychological screening program was found to amount to a maximum of 0.73. The specificity was estimated at 0.98 to 0.99 and the predictive positive value at 0.67. The conclusion drawn from the study was that the effectiveness of the screening program was sufficiently high to motivate a continuation of the procedure.

THE SCREENING PROGRAM

To demonstrate whether the goals of the screening program have been achieved, the evaluation must include a long-term follow-up study. In 1975 a project was started in Uppsala with the aim to elucidate the importance of the systematic health-screening of 4-year-olds for the state of health at the age of 10. The crucial question was whether the prevalence of health problems was lower in a group of children who had undergone the screening diagnosis and treatment, as compared with a group of children who had not had that opportunity.

Material and Methods

The health screening of 4-year-olds started gradually in the year 1969, with children born in 1965. The CHCs were included successively, and from the beginning of the year 1971, all CHCs were included. This means that only a fraction of the children born in 1965 and 1966 was eligible for the control group. Originally, it was intended to compare all children who had had the opportunity to participate with all those who had not, but it was soon found that the selection of CHCs in the first 2 years had not been made at random. Therefore, it was necessary to perform a matching on the level of the child-health district. The result of the matching process finally was that it led to the creation of one quasi-experimental group of children ($N = 1,112$) born in 1967 and a control group ($N = 947$) of children born in 1965. The groups were comparable in terms of geographical area and trimester of birth. There was no significant change in the epidemiological situation between 1969 and 1971, and the basic Child Health Care offered to the children before the age of 4 was the same in both groups. There were some changes, however, in that new housing estates were populated between 1969 and 1971; but only a fraction of the children was affected by this migration, so the effect on the composition of the samples must have been negligible. Concerning background variables in the quasi-experimental group and the control group, there were no differences with respect to sex, size of school, location of school, and "image of school" from a psycho-social point of view.

Data related to the children's health and adaptation in school were compiled by means of interviews with school teachers and school nurses. The interviews were made in Grade 3 (spring term); by this time the children usually have had the same teacher from the school entrance and, thus, are well known by the school. Depending on early or delayed school entrance, 3.1% of the children were found to be in Grade 2 and 2.4% in Grade 4. The interviews were made by specially trained, ex-perienced nurses.

The nurse gave the following data about the children: weight and height, visual acuity in Grades 1 and 4, time of detection of visual disorder, result of hearing test (audiogram) in Grades 1 and 4, handicap or specific chronic disease, psychological problems known by nurse (slight, moderate, or severe: aggressiveness, anxiety, dependence, hy-peractivity, lack of concentration, peer problems, other psychological problems), social family problems, consultations with specialists from 7 to 10 years of age, hospital admissions, dispensation from gymnastics.

The interview with the teacher included: handicap or chronic disease known by teacher, general ability, dyslexia, speech problems, gross motor ability, fine motor ability, special schooling and instruction, psy-chological problems known by teacher (same problems as for nurse interview), social problems in the family known by teacher.

Finally, the study was supplemented with a special follow-up of the records of those eight children who had had the most serious health problems detected through the screening program. The purpose of this last phase was to analyze whether some children had had a great benefit, perhaps in the form of life-saving therapy, through the detection of a health problem and referral.

The comparison between the experimental group and the control group was performed using 56 health variables based on the interview data. The statistical differences were evaluated using the X^2 test. With respect to the number of comparisions and sample size, only differences at $p \leq 0.025$ were accepted as significant.

Results

The study group differed from the control group with respect to: lower frequency of overweight, lower age of detection of visual disorders, fewer children in special class but more children with some sort of therapeutic instruction, higher frequency of hospital admissions, higher number of unspecified psychological problems. With the exception of the lower rate of overweight, the differences will probably be revealed to depend on methodological bias. The difference of 2 years between the experimental group and the control group obviously has created some evaluation problems. In any case, these findings, difficult to interpret, are not further discussed in this context. For the overwhelming majority of health variables, no difference between the experimental and the control group was found. Scrutinization of the records of the eight children with previously unknown serious health problems showed that most of the children probably had received some benefit from the therapeutic measures but that the screening was not decisive for any child's fate.

DISCUSSION

The general conclusion of this analysis is that with the measures obtained on 10-year-olds in this study, it has hardly been possible to detect any beneficial effect of the health screening. The measures used in this study are admittedly crude and incomplete, but they reflect most of the true problems suffered by school-children of this age. Although the health screening has not contributed to the prevention of most problems to a statistically significant degree, the possibility cannot be excluded that there may have been other beneficial effects not covered by the data collected. Thus, it has not been possible to include information provided by the parents. It is well-known that children may exhibit different problem behaviors at home and in school. It is necessary to admit that the difference of 2 years between the quasi-experimental group and the control group may have caused fallacies. There is good reason, however, to believe that these problems are not severe enough to invalidate the main conclusion of the comparison between the two samples, namely that the health screening of 4-year-old children has contributed little to the general state of health of 10-year-old children. Several explanations for this negative and unexpected result are possible.

Participation in the screening was about 98%, and the few nonparticipants did not show the attributes of a high-risk group. Therefore, this explanation can be excluded a priori. Left are the following five main alternatives:

Most of those long-lasting health problems in which early treatment is essential had already been detected before the age of 4.

The screening itself is effective, the treatments are not effective or not performed at all.

The screening and treatments of the children in the experiment group were effective; but parents, preschool teachers, etc., using informal methods, were equally effective in detecting health problems in need of treatment in the control group.

The screening methods were not valid, or their application in the routine health-care situation was not appropriate.

The precursors of the 10-year-olds' health problems cannot be identified effectively by screening at age 4, because the state of health undergoes important changes between 4 and 10 years of age, under the influences of environmental factors.

The conclusions concerning future preventive strategies will differ widely depending on which of these explanations is considered most likely. A unique decision for one or another of these alternatives will probably not be possible, but we believe that further analysis of our data will render it possible to make statements concerning their relative importance. The evaluation is ongoing and will continue with studies of the predictive values of the screening program and with an analysis of the social determinants of changes in health in the interval between 4 and 10 years of age.

REFERENCES

Nilsson, C., Sundelin, C., and Vuille, J-C. 1976. General health screening of four-year-olds in a Swedish county. IV. An analysis of the effectiveness of the psychological examination program. Acta Paediatr. Scand. 65:663.

Sundelin, C., and Vuille, J-C. 1976. Health screening of four-year-olds in a Swedish county. III. Variation of effectiveness among examining teams. Acta Paediatr. Scand. 65:193.

Sundelin, C., and Vuille, J-C. 1975. Health screening of four-year-olds in a Swedish county. II. Effectiveness in detecting health problems. Acta Paediatr. Scand. 64:801.

Sundelin, C., and Vuille, J-C. 1975. Health screening of four-year-olds in a Swedish county. I. Organization, methods and participation. Acta Paediatr. Scand. 64:795.

Chapter 12

The Metro-Manila Developmental Screening Test (MMDST):

A Normative Study

Phoebe D. Williams

Preventive medicine is a special concern in public health, and developmental screening for the early detection of disability in children is part of this concern. In order to be able to do any developmental screening, however, norms of development first have to be established. The study described in this chapter was conducted to develop norms for the Denver Developmental Screening Test on Metro-Manila children (hereafter to be known as the Metro-Manila Developmental Screening Test—MMDST) and to determine the characteristics of low-scoring (abnormal and questionable) and high-scoring (normal) children on the developmental screening test.

The normative study of the Metro-Manila Developmental Screening Test (MMDST) was funded by the National Science Development Board and the University of the Philippines Integrated Research Program (Project No. 7703 So) with the author as project Leader. Co-researcher in the project was Professor Adeline B. Abad-Santos, R.N., M.A. Data collection was done mainly by Aida Fajatin, Edna Guardian, Beverly Lucena, and Rizalina Tuason, all registered nurses. Statistical analysis was done by Arthur R. Williams, Ph.D.

149

THE STUDY

Setting and Subjects

The study was done in six of the 17 municipalities making up Metro-Manila (Quezon City, Manila, Marikina, San Juan, Venezuela, and Makati). The subjects were 6,006 normal children between the ages of 2 weeks and 6½ years. The study excluded children who exhibited the following: premature birth and low birthweight; twin, breech, or cesarean section delivery; handicaps of vision, hearing, walking, speaking, or the central nervous system; present weights less than the 10th percentile or more than the 90th percentile of established weight standards. Children who were illegitimate or from broken families were also excluded.

Sampling

A combination multistage, cluster (with implicit stratification), systematic, and quota sampling (Babbie, 1974) was done. Multistage sampling involved the following sampling stages arranged in order: municipality/city, district/zone, barangay, households, and, finally, children below 6½ years of age. No more than three children per household were tested and 4,846 households were included by systematic sampling. Quota sampling was based on the child's age and sex, the father's occupation and education, and the sampling site.

Seventy-five age groupings (Frankenburg and Dodds, 1967) and ten occupational groupings (National Census and Statistics Office, 1975) were used. Father's education was categorized into college, high school, and elementary. Because many upper and middle class households refused household sampling, they were eventually reached through 15 doctors' clinics and five preschools ($N = 830$). A profile of the occupational-group distribution of the sample children's fathers in comparison with those of Metro-Manila and the entire country is given in Table 1.

The original materials and 105 items of the Denver Developmental Screening Test (DDST) were slightly modified. The method of test administration was closely patterned after that of Frankenburg et al. (1970). Four research assistants worked full time, and research aides helped in data collection and analysis. Intensive training, reliability testing, and close monitoring of data collectors were done.

Test Reliability

Interrater reliability ($N = 150$), test-retest reliability ($N = 130$), and mother-tester reliability ($N = 160$) were done at the start of the study. Total agreement on all three ranged between 96% and 97%. Individual item analysis on the three measures of reliability was also done (Williams, 1980c) with satisfactory results comparable to those reported by Frank-

Table 1. A profile of the occupational group distributions (in percentages) for the entire Philippine and Metro-Manila populations age 10 years and above and for the sample children's fathers

Occupational groups	Percentage distribution		
	Philippines	Metro-Manila	Sample
Professionals, technical workers	5.0	9.5	11.8
Proprietors, managers, administrators	0.9	3.3	5.0
Clerical workers	3.7	13.5	14.8
Sales workers	9.8	12.9	8.7
Farmers, fishermen, loggers	55.6	2.0	1.0
Transport and communication workers	3.6	8.6	11.2
Craftsmen and production-process workers	10.8	25.3	25.1
Manual workers and laborers	1.8	2.3	16.6
Service and related workers	8.2	20.6	1.1
Occupation not reported	0.2	2.0	4.7
Workers in mines and quarries	0.2		
Total	100.0	100.0	100.0

National Census and Statistical Office, 1975.

enburg et al. (1971) and Werner and Bayley (1966). Test-retest agreement on items passed by report (range 75.3%–100%; mean 87.6%) did not vary appreciably from agreement on items not passable by report (range 80%–100%; mean 90.0%). Tester-observer agreement on items passed by report (range 89.7%–100%; mean 98.4%) did not vary appreciably from agreement on items not passable by report (range 88.6%–100%; mean 97.7%). Finally, mother-tester agreement on items passable by report (range 78.8%–100%; mean 97.1%) varied considerably from items not passable by report (range 64.4%–100%; mean 89.2).

Test Validity

Two sets of data on the concurrent validity of the test are available. First, the test was used in two pediatric specialty clinics (neurology and endocrine-metabolic) on patients with diagnoses of post-encephalitis/meningitis, cerebral palsy, or hypothyroidism. All children tested were found to be retarded.

Second, the test was validated against the Gesell test. The MMDST and Gesell were administered to 269 children within a week interval, and the mental ages and developmental quotients were correlated using the Pearson correlation technique. The 90% Pass method (Frankenburg et al. 1971, p. 477) was used to determine mental age on the MMDST. The results showed a high correlation (0.97) between the two tests. The four sectors of the test were likewise highly correlated (Layug, 1980).

The Gesell test was used because one local study (Valenzuela et al. 1969) showed that motor and adaptive development of Filipino children compared well with American norms on the Gesell test, although delays were noted in language and personal-social development. Valenzuela's longitudinal study was done on middle/upper class children up to the fifth year of life and is the closest semblance of a normative study done locally that is appropriate for children below 6 years. Philippine-made tests or restandardizations of foreign tests are few. Of those available, none are appropriate for children in the 0–6 years age range.

Regarding predictive validity, scores on the MMDST (MMDST-1) of 178 children were correlated with: 1) the same children's MMDST scores approximately 2 years later (MMDST-2); or 2) if they were older than 6½ years, with their scores on the Philippine Nonverbal Intelligence Test (PNIT); and 3) their average school grade. The Pearson correlation coefficients showed considerable consistency between first and second MMDST testing ($r = 0.77$; $p < 0.001$) after an interval of 2 years. The 90% Pass method was also used to determine mental age on the MMDST. MMDST-1 and average school grade correlated 0.28 ($p < 0.05$); a higher correlation was obtained between the MMDST-1 fine motor-adaptive sector and average school grade ($r = 0.40$; $p < 0.01$). MMDST-1 and PNIT correlated 0.41 ($p < 0.01$); a higher correlation was also obtained between the MMDST-1 fine motor-adaptive sector and the PNIT ($r = 0.42$; $p < 0.01$) (Williams, 1980d). Additional studies on the concurrent and predictive validity of the MMDST need to be done and on a larger scale than those done thus far.

Data Analysis

Probit analysis was used to compute the ages at which 25%, 50%, 75%, and 90% of the children passed each of the 105 test items. This was done overall as well as separately for boys and girls and for children of college-, high school-, and elementary-educated fathers. Father's education was used as a gauge of family socioeconomic status.

Discriminant analysis was done to determine the characteristics of high-scoring and low-scoring children in the normative population of the MMDST. High-scoring children were those whose scores were normal on the MMDST. Low-scoring children were those whose scores were questionable or abnormal. Standardized discriminant weights can be given the same interpretation as standardized regression coefficients (Kelly et al. (1969). Coefficients above 0.20 were considered significant, below this level were trends. Forty-five independent variables were used in this present analysis.

Descriptive analysis of the normative children's figure drawings was also done to illustrate the principle of individuality among children (Abad Santos, 1980). Results of that analysis, however, are not reported here.

RESULTS

Probit analysis established the overall norms for the MMDST, and a test form was constructed for test administration purposes on the basis of these norms. The analysis also established norms for boys and girls and for children whose fathers level of education was college, high school, and elementary school. Performance of children of college-educated fathers was significantly better on a majority of the items compared to performance of children of elementary- and high-school-educated fathers. Compared to boys, nonsignificant gains were seen in the performance of girls.

Using the Z-statistic to compare the ages at which the DDST items were passed by 50% of the Denver sample and the ages at which the MMDST items were passed by 50% of the Metro-Manila sample, it was found that the majority of the items on all behavior sectors was obtained significantly earlier by the Denver sample (Williams, 1980b, p. 178). These figures are given in Table 2.

Discriminant analysis showed four clusters of factors as significantly associated with children's performance. Heaviest discriminant coefficients were associated with caregiving factors or variables directly related to the care of the child. The results suggested that if the mother-substitute caregiver was older, and the longer she had resided in Metro-Manila, the more likely the child was to be normal on the test. Data showed that if the mother was not the caregiver of the child, the most common mother-substitute was a maid (nannie) or a grandmother (lola).

A second cluster of variables that also emerged as important centered on the mother herself, her level of education, and to a lesser extent, her birth place. The higher the mother's level of education, the more likely the child was to have a normal score on the test. There was also a trend indicating that mothers born in an urban area tended to have children with normal scores.

Table 2.   Number of items per sector that Metro-Manila children attained significantly later, earlier, and about the same median age, compared to the Denver sample

Metro-Manila Children	Behavior sector			
	Gross motor	Fine motor adaptive	Language	Personal social
Number of items attained significantly later	20	22	17	14
Number of items attained significantly earlier	3	1	1	5
Number of differences	6	5	1	2
Total (97)	29	28	19	21

A third cluster of variables that were important centered on the child and certain situational factors. Altogether, the variables seemed to favor a younger family with fewer children and greater spacing between children.

A fourth cluster of variables that received substantial discriminant weights seemed to point to the fact that the test was more sensitive to the performance of the older child. This is considered a test artifact that merits further investigation.

DISCUSSION

Considering the clusters of factors found to correlate with low or high performance on the MMDST, the implications clearly point to the home environment. The provision of classes for mothers and mother-substitutes that include aspects on child health, growth, and development are particularly useful. It should be pointed out that when one talks about "caregivers" in the Philippines, there is an extended family context. Caregivers include relatives and older female children who may be given child-care responsibilities when the mother is engaged in economic activities. Therefore, improvement in the training of mother-substitutes must be directed toward high- and middle-income families that hire helpers as well as toward lower income households that operate within an extended family system. In this regard, a program like FEED (Anastasiow et al. 1977) might be worked out in school curricula (such as in the home economics course in grades 5 and 6) to target older female children and other substitute caregivers who may be given child-caregiving responsibilities eventually.

In addition, the importance of keeping family size small and child spacing wider must be emphasized. Making preschool education more accessible to the poorer segments of society would be helpful. As yet, with a few exceptions, preschools are privately run and available only to those with higher socioeconomic status.

In cases in which the child has been identified as developmentally delayed, the most realistic intervention in the well-child-care context is that of pointing out to the mother or her substitute ways of ameliorating the situation. For example, in cases of language delays, focus may be made on the importance of verbal stimulation in the form of naming objects, describing how things work and function, answering the child's questions, and verbal responsiveness in general. At present, early cognitive and language stimulation is not considered important by many Filipino mothers.

Expectations for school performance in grade one, which begins at age 7 in the Philippines, include the ability to read and write. Without some intervention during the preschool period, such as the above examples, this expectation is difficult to fulfill. As one source has aptly said: "the roots of learning are formed long before a child enters first grade; but it is a tragic fact that in the case of large numbers of children—the have-nots in the world—these roots are blighted before they begin their school careers" (Grant, 1973). In the Philippines this is seen as a priority area. In 1981, programs on preschool education and early identification of growth and developmental disabilities are to be launched. At the same time efforts will be continued toward population control and the improvement of nutrition among preschool children. International agencies like UNICEF and USAID have been helpful.

In the Philippines, as in most developing countries, the primary problem is stringent resource constraints. Some of the information and ideas presented in this chapter suggest changes in the focus of health care delivery that do not necessarily require huge increases in expenditures. For example, an increased emphasis on mother and mother-substitute training could be done within existing community health centers with little increase in cost. Developmental screening could be done by nurses and midwives as part of their regular activities thereby enlarging both the number of persons who conduct screening and the number of children screened. Such efforts would do much to assist children in need early in their lives.

REFERENCES

Abad Santos, A. 1980. An analysis of figure drawing of Metro-Manila preschool children. In: P. Williams (ed.), Development of Norms for the Denver Developmental Screening Test on Metro-Manila Children 0–6 Years Old, pp. 115–198. NSDB-UPS(A) Project 7703 So.

Anastasiow, N., Grimmett, S., Eggleston, P., and Brown, J. 1977. Facilitative Environments Encouraging Development (FEED). Institute for Child Study, Indiana University, Bloomington.

Babbie, E. 1974. Survey Research Methods. Wadsworth, Belmont, CA.

Frankenburg, W., and Dodds, J. 1967. Denver Developmental Screening Test Manual. University of Colorado Press, Denver.

Frankenburg, W., Goldstein, A., Chabot, A., Camp. B. W., and Fitch, M. 1970. Training the Indigenous Nonprofessional: The Screening Technician. J. Pediatrics, 77:564–570.

Frankenburg, W. K., Camp, B. W., and VanNatta, P. A. 1971. Validity of the Denver Developmental Screening Test. Child Dev. 42:475–485.

Grant, D. R. B. 1973. A Better Education Start for Jamaica's Children. The Neglected Years: Early Childhood, UNICEF.

Kelly, F. J., et al. 1969. Multiple Regression Approach: Research Design for the Behavioral Sciences. Southern Illinois University, Carbondale.

Layug, E. 1980. Concurrent validation of the DDST (Metro-Manila version). Unpublished master's thesis, University of the Philippines, Quezon City.

National Census and Statistics Office. 1975. Reports. Republic of the Philippines. 1979. A Study on the Situation of Children in the Philippines: Summary. Manila.

Valenzuela, Amanda et. al. Growth and developmental norms of Filipino children, NSDB, Project 286, 1969.

Werner, E. E., and Bayley, N. 1966. The Reliability of Bayley's Revised Scale of Mental and Motor Development During the First Year of Life. Child Dev. 37:39–50.

Williams, P. D. 1980a. The Development of Norms for the Denver Developmental Screening Test on Metro-Manila Children, 0–6 Years Old. NSDB-UPS(A) Project No. 7703 So.

Williams, P. D. 1980b. A comparative study of DDST norms developed in five locales. In: P. D. Williams (Ed.), Nursing Research in the Philippines: A Sourcebook. JMC Press, Quezon City.

Williams, P. D. 1980c. The reliability of the Denver Developmental Screening Test: Metro-Manila version. In: P. Williams (Ed.), Development of Norms for the Denver Developmental Screening Test on Metro-Manila Children, 0–6 Years Old. NSDB-UPS(A) Project No. 7703 So., Appendix J.

Williams, P. D. 1980d. Predictive Validity of the Metro-Manila Developmental Screening Test. Paper presented at the Philippine Psychological Association Convention, August 26, Manila.

Williams, P. D. 1979. Children at Risk: Perinatal Events and Their Effects on Development: A Cross-Sectional Study. Unpublished preliminary analysis.

Chapter 13

Auditing Multidisciplinary Assessment Procedures:

A System Developed for the Brookline Early Education Project

Donald E. Pierson, Melvin D. Levine,
Ruth Wolman

The Brookline Early Education Project (BEEP) is a longitudinal research and demonstration program operated by a public school system. The major goal of the project has been to determine the benefits of comprehensive early education, an approach that has entailed three related strategies:

Health and developmental surveillance
Parent education
Educational programs for children

The health and developmental surveillance involved periodic exams conducted on eight occasions between 2 weeks of age and entry to

This report was made possible by funds granted by Carnegie Corporation of New York and The Robert Wood Johnson Foundation. The statements made and views expressed are solely the responsibility of the authors.

kindergarten. Each child's health and developmental growth were carefully followed, and indications for specialized attention or referral were coordinated closely with primary care providers.

The parent education was offered within certain cost limitations; it included options for home visits, parent-group meetings, a book and toy lending library, classroom observations, social work outreach, and informal discussion. These contacts served to inform, support, and advocate for parents so that the parents would become active partners with professionals in the process of ensuring the children's health and educational growth.

The educational programs for children consisted of weekly playgroups at age 2 years and a daily prekindergarten program at ages 3 and 4 years. These provided enriching experiences as well as specific plans for developmental needs identified for each child. The goal was to prevent relatively minor or precursor problems from leading to more serious difficulties (such as hyperactivity, learning disabilities, social interaction problems, and underachievement) by mobilizing treatment and support networks before the child entered elementary school.

To monitor the diagnostic and intervention process, an auditing system called the Longitudinal Study of Findings was developed. Forms and protocols were designed to characterize the nature of findings, coordinate recommendations for follow-up, supervise implementation of services, and evaluate outcomes. The audit was first applied when the children reached 42 months of age. By this time a substantial amount of background and early developmental data had been collected on each child. There was also reason to suspect more stability in findings than would have been likely at earlier points (Levine et al., 1977). Furthermore, by this time in the pilot project, the educational intervention strategies had been refined and carefully articulated. Consequently, for practical and theoretical reasons, the auditing system was implemented at age 42 months and continued to kindergarten entry.

This chapter considers the utility of auditing the multidisciplinary assessment procedures by addressing five questions:

1. What findings emerged regarding the children served by the project at age 42 months?
2. What proportion of these findings at 42 months led to recommendations for intervention by the resources available in the project and in the community?
3. How many of the recommendations were actually implemented?
4. To what extent were the findings at age 42 months judged as ameliorated at the time of entry into kindergarten?

5.   How did parents value the periodic health and developmental exams in general?

METHOD

Enrollment in BEEP began 3 months prior to the birth of a child and was open to families residing in the town of Brookline and adjacent neighborhoods in the city of Boston. The one condition on enrollment was that the family should have no plans to move in the foreseeable future. Although participation was thus not contingent upon being "at risk," the project made a strong commitment to enlist families who might need help but who would not seek out such a program. For instance, social service agencies, health clinics, school personnel, and especially parents recruited many families who ordinarily would not volunteer for such a program (Nicol, 1978). By the time the project reached its quota of 285 families in the fall of 1974, a rather diverse group had been assembled. The mothers' ages at the births of the children ranged from 14 to 39 years, with a median of 28 years. About one-half of the mothers were college graduates. Sexes of the children were fairly evenly represented (53% male, 47% female). About 60% of the children were white, about one-fourth were black, and the remainder were of Hispanic and Oriental descent. By age 42 months, 229 children had been enrolled in BEEP continuously from birth. Nearly all of the families who had left the program had moved from the area. The demographic characteristics of the sample were not altered significantly by this attrition.

The age 42-month assessment consisted of several components. First, a nurse conducted a health history interview with one or both parents. The interview covered recent illnesses, nature and consistency of health care, family stresses, and parent concerns about the child's health and development. Next, a psychologist administered the McCarthy Scales of Children's Abilities. Then, on a separate occasion, a pediatrician administered vision and hearing screening tests, a neurodevelopmental examination (Levine and Oberklaid, 1977), and a traditional physical and neurologic examination. Concurrently, teachers who knew the child from a prekindergarten classroom setting reported any concerns they might have and solicited reactions and concerns of the parents.

Shortly after these data were gathered, a team meeting composed of teachers, psychologists, and medical personnel was convened to pool and discuss the independently documented observations. Each "finding," or potential concern, was recorded according to criteria defined in a detailed manual (Wolman, Yurchak, and Levine, 1980). Inclusion of nonhealth findings was contingent upon reports from two or more members of the team; health findings were included if identified by the medical representative. Each finding was rated by consensus for its severity (great, moderate, mild, undetermined), its prescriptive implications (i.e., treatability), and its predictive value (i.e., potential impact on future behavior and academic performance).

For purposes of analysis, the findings were classified into the following six general categories.

Health findings were assembled from medical histories, physical examinations, and sensory assessments. Excluded from this tabulation were acute, self-limited conditions, such as transient upper-respiratory infections and trivial injuries.

Developmental delays were identified on the basis of standardized tests (e.g., scale indices of one or more standard deviations below mean for age on McCarthy Scale) coupled with a consensus of clinical judgments by examiners, teachers, and parents. Developmental areas included language, speech, perceptual-motor skill, quantitative ability, overall cognitive development, memory, and motor function.

Behavioral organization findings were defined as signs of dysfunction likely to interfere with a child's ability to acquire skills, conform to routines, and interact meaningfully. Findings in this area were described by teachers and parents as difficulties in concentrating on activities in the classroom or home and by examiners as the inability to sustain attention during the individual exams.

Social-emotional findings included difficulties in relating to adults, problems with peer interaction, and undue expressions of anxiety, depression, aggression, or fearfulness.

Critical events referred to incidents or new life-situations occurring within 1 year prior to the 42-months checkpoint and thought to have the potential to impair a child's behavior, learning, or health. Included were major illnesses in the child or family, hospitalizations, deaths of close relatives, changes of residence, births of siblings, parental separations, or episodes of abuse or other violence.

Chronic environmental concerns encompassed persistent stresses in the child's home or daily-care setting: poor nutrition, inadequate housing, alcoholism, chronic family health problems, inability to attend school regularly.

Specific interventions were then tailored to fit each child's configuration of findings. Strengths of the child and family as well as availability of resources were taken into account in formulating the plan. Educational programs for children and for parents were implemented by BEEP teachers, utilizing strategies outlined in the BEEP Prekindergarten Curriculum

(Hauser-Cram and Pierson, 1980). Noneducational interventions included various referrals for further consultation, health and developmental counseling, as well as social services. With parent approval, referrals to outside agencies and to school personnel were coordinated and expedited by BEEP staff. In some cases it was decided that, despite findings, no recommendations were warranted. All recommendations and actions were recorded on specially designed forms.

Figure 1 illustrates the auditing process: intake of findings from direct observation and historical data, designation of individual ratings (severity, prescriptive, and predictive), formulation of recommendations, monitoring for compliance, and the assignment of outcome ratings at entry into kindergarten.

To supplement the documentation and evaluation of findings, parents were asked to evaluate the project components by responding to a questionnaire before the child entered kindergarten.

RESULTS

Findings and Severity Ratings

A total of 784 findings were tabulated from the 229 children. One hundred ninety-nine of the children (87%) had at least one finding, and the majority had more than two such notations. The impression that most of these findings fell within limits conventionally regarded as normal was confirmed by reference to summary scores of the Denver Development Screening Test: 94% of the scores were rated as "normal," 5% as "questionable," and 1% as "abnormal."

The health area accounted for more findings than any other single area. The most prevalent health findings were orthopedic defects (abnormalities of gait and foot structure), ear diseases (primarily chronic serious otitis), hearing loss, heart murmurs, and lowered visual acuity. Speech and language difficulties predominated among the developmental delays. Only 28 of the 208 developmental findings were judged to be of great severity. There was also a considerable number (95) of findings in the behavioral-organization category, with the majority of these judged as mild or moderate. In the social-emotional area, difficulty in relating to adults was the most frequently cited finding; again, most findings in this area were rated "moderate" in severity. Most of the 38 critical events recorded for the children in the preceding year, notably the birth of siblings, were judged to be of undetermined severity. Unlike findings in the other areas, environmental concerns, when they occurred, were skewed toward great severity; more than half of these findings received such ratings.

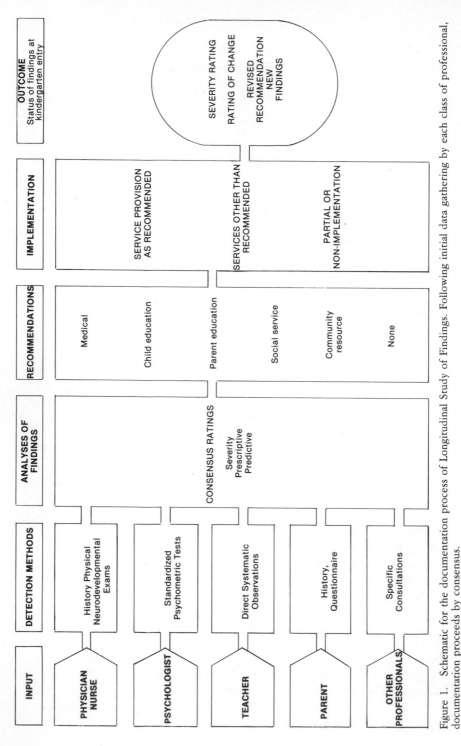

Figure 1. Schematic for the documentation process of Longitudinal Study of Findings. Following initial data gathering by each class of professional, documentation proceeds by consensus.

162

Prescriptive Ratings and Recommendations

The proportion of findings amenable to available treatments was calculated by staff consensus on a 5-point scale: high, moderate, minimal, none, and undetermined. Overall, 15% of the findings received a high prescriptive rating. The largest proportion of these was in the health area, where 22% were rated as highly conducive to successful intervention. It is interesting to note that high prescriptive ratings were seldom given in the category of developmental delay. Overall, 23% of the findings were regarded as having no prescriptive implications, and another 12% could not be assigned a rating because of a lack of staff consensus.

Recommendations for action were formulated by the multidisciplinary team on a child basis, taking into account all aspects of the individual child's functioning, rather than on a finding basis. Consistent with the project's orientation that parents are the child's most important teachers, specific recommendations were most often made for the category of parent education. Recommendations for child's program and parent education were generally coordinated with each other. Regarding the project's intention to tailor programs to the individual needs of children, the staff actually recommended individualization for 68% of the children following the 42-month exam.

Compliance

Implementation of the original recommendation or an appropriate modification was achieved in a high percentage of cases. The greatest difficulty in attaining compliance was experienced in the area of social work support; seven families with overwhelming economic burdens and a history of inadequate institutional response could not be engaged in a continuous program during this period of time.

Outcome Judgments

At the conclusion of the BEEP preschool program, 1½ to 2 years after the 42-month assessments, staff reassembled to take stock of the effectiveness of the individually-tailored interventions. About two-thirds of the findings reflected some progress. Optimal progress, indicating that the finding was no longer apparent, was achieved on 36% of all findings. The remaining findings, however, persisted: 31%, some—but less than optimal—progress; 28%, no progress; and 6%, increased concerns. Nearly one-half of the health findings were recorded as showing optimal progress. Critical events, as one would expect by definition, seldom recurred during the ensuing period.

It is of interest to note that moderate- and mild-severity findings showed more progress across all finding categories than did great-severity findings. Indeed, in the behavioral-organization area, none of the 23 great-severity findings showed optimal progress, and only 3 of the 26 environmental findings of great severity reflected optimal progress in spite of intervention.

Parents' Reactions

Figure 2 summarizes questionnaire results, showing that parents rated the health and developmental exams very favorably. In fact, many parents commented that the exams were the single most valuable component in BEEP. When asked to elaborate on their feelings, parents indicated that it was not simply the exam report or the parents' observations of the exam (although these were generally viewed in a favorable manner) but rather the informal discussion afterward that was so valued. Parents did acknowledge anxieties in anticipation of the diagnostic scrutiny (e.g., "I wondered if my child would cooperate and whether the experts would think I was doing a good job"). These worries were offset by the empathic

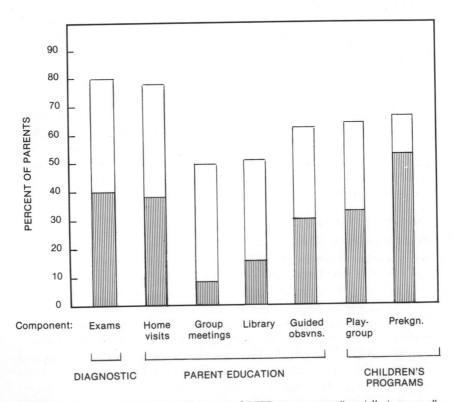

Figure 2.   Parent ratings of the importance of BEEP components: "crucially important" (cross-hatched areas) and "important but not crucial" (white areas).

manner in which impressions about the child's functioning were exchanged. The opportunity to gain understanding and reassurance about all aspects of their child's health and development was often felt to be lacking in the primary care setting. If parents had questions, they felt the BEEP diagnostic staff could give them the time and the information necessary to allay anxieties and build confidence.

DISCUSSION

A strikingly high yield of diagnostic findings was documented at the age of 42 months. This might be surprising in view of the fact that a "normal" population was under scrutiny. Moreover, these preschoolers had been monitored and had received interventions since birth. A similar analysis undertaken in a setting where fewer resources are available might result in a very different yield of service needs.

Clearly, these findings are not synonymous with "pathology" or even being "at risk." Rather, many of the findings represent indicators of vulnerability and issues for individualized monitoring or anticipatory counseling. Certain clusters may have power for predicting later school problems. Other findings may reflect no immediate or long-term significance. Recognition of this broad diagnostic range is an essential refinement for preventive approaches to education and pediatrics (Oberklaid, Dworkin, and Levine, 1979).

There is ample evidence of a constant interplay between categories of findings within a child. For example, environmental stresses are apt to aggravate weak attention or ineffective learning in school. Developmental delays may precipitate or exacerbate "hyperactivity" and motivational problems in a classroom. On the other hand, delays may be offset by certain child and family strengths or by an appropriately structured classroom situation.

The Longitudinal Study of Findings enhanced the staff's awareness of these synergistic processes. Formulation, documentation, and plans for intervention depended upon the multidisciplinary pooling and analysis of observations. For example, one child came from a home where there was considerable family strife. He also had episodes of recurrent otitis media and evidence of a language disability likely to impair behavior and learning in school. Special teacher attention or compliance in medical treatment for the child's recurrent otitis media might have been futile unless the family was helped to cope with environmental stresses simultaneously.

The Longitudinal Study of Findings uncovered needs that have implications for planning other preventive childhood programs. In the health area, the highest yield of findings occurred within the subspecialties of orthopedics and otolaryngology. Future projects should place particular emphasis on health assessments that include systematic diagnostic attention to these areas. In particular, the high yield of middle-ear and auditory-acuity problems might argue for widespread application of sophisticated techniques, such as tympanometry.

In the developmental area, the high occurrence of language problems suggests the need for meticulous scrutiny of this area. All educators and pediatricians who work with young children should be well trained to assess and deal with the often subtle disabilities affecting language.

It is important to point out that service implications will differ in various settings and with various populations. The high rate of compliance with service recommendations was attained by specific role responsibilities and with frequent communication among the multidisciplinary staff. This rate was surely facilitated by the generally adequate socioeconomic resources of most of the families, but it also hinged upon the trusting relationships built between staff and families from the time of the child's birth.

In this study the apparent stabilization of relatively severe problems from age 42 months to entry into kindergarten raises questions for further research. In light of these results, one should temper promises about how much impact school-based programs can have on severe problems of the 42-month-old child. On the other hand, it is encouraging that at least some progress was judged for more than two-thirds of problems in the primary purview of educators, that is, those categorized here as developmental, behavioral-organization, and social-emotional. This rate of progress suggests an impact that is greater than could be expected by maturation or spontaneous remission.

It is submitted that, as a system for auditing the individual assessment and delivery of human services, a procedure such as the Longitudinal Study of Findings can be useful. When there are constraints of cost containment, this process can help to establish priorities (Sanazaro et al., 1972). For instance, some policymakers may believe that early childhood services should focus their resources exclusively on children who have findings with high prescriptive ratings. That is to say, energies should be channeled toward conditions likely to be remediable. Assessment techniques that do not uncover correctable findings might be deemphasized or even eliminated.

In a project the major aim of which is prevention, one might *not* wish to allocate substantial resources toward the abatement of findings that are likely to have little impact on the child's future functioning. In the most parsimonious of cases, one might want to plan services around yields of findings that are both reasonably predictive and prescriptive, perhaps adding to this the stipulation that findings be either moderate or severe. Such diagnostic distillation can become an ongoing process through which service priorities can be questioned and revised when necessary.

The Longitudinal Study of Findings in itself can enhance services. Within the Brookline Early Education Project it has served as a focal point for interdisciplinary discussion. Professionals have been forced to incorporate parents in the planning and to justify decisions concerning findings and the distribution of limited services. It was found, as others have indicated (Wise, Rubin, and Beckard, 1974; Holm and McCartin, 1978), that discrepant perspectives between disciplines can be argued systematically and usually resolved by consensus. The process of attempting to isolate findings in individual children, then examining the ways in which these interact within the same child, facilitated and strengthened the coordination of services. In this way, it was possible to introduce a system for documenting service activity while applying the same procedure in promoting diagnostic accountability and quality assurance (Simeonsson and Wiegerink, 1975). By defining and recording findings and recommendations, it became almost impossible for specific needs to "fall between the cracks" or become lost in the day-to-day "housekeeping" operations of the program.

In addition to early education, systems such as the Longitudinal Study of Findings might be applied to health maintenance organizations, neighborhood health centers, and physicians' offices. A systematic audit also could be applied as part of the formulation of individual education plans under Public Law 94-142, the Special Education Act (Palfrey, Mervis, and Butler, 1978). Perhaps some adaptation for quality control in public programs such as Head Start (Smith and Bissell, 1970) and Project Good Health, formerly EPSDT (Dixon, 1974), might prove useful.

The large majority of parents in this study found the diagnostic surveillance to be helpful, primarily because it gave them a chance to have their questions answered and to feel better informed about their child's health and development. This is consistent with Starfield's and Barkowe's (1969) finding that one-half of the questions about the child's behavior raised by mothers in well-child visits were not dealt with or even acknowledged. Also, Baker, Lister, and Milhaus (1976) noted that 97% of the patients in a comprehensive health-care center indicated they worried less when time was taken to fully inform them about the results of an examination. Observation and discussion of the child's BEEP exam performances gave parents an opportunity to understand the context of broad developmental norms, temperamental styles, and situational factors that precipitate certain behaviors by the child. Harmful labels and superstitious explanations for behavior could be dispelled.

Certainly, analysis of the properties of findings raises many questions. Was harm done by overidentification? Were findings with high predictive ratings modified in some way to improve later child outcomes? Did the process of analyzing findings itself result in better treatment for children? Could we catalog positive findings and ecological measures in a complementary way? How expensive are this scrutiny and coordination? Is the kind of data generated by the Longitudinal Study of Findings useful for public-policy planners?

Objective outcome and intensive process studies are required to answer these questions. Several are now under way within the Brookline Early Education Project. Ultimately, it would be helpful if the documentation and evaluation methods could be refined and standardized so that comparable data are available from service programs in other settings. Such advances could facilitate a fruitful exchange of ideas and more widespread replication of effective diagnostic and educational models.

CONCLUSION

Periodic health and developmental exams coupled with educational resources and an auditing system represents one approach to monitoring the child's development. In this approach, the process of auditing is as important as the product; the specific count of findings here is not so pertinent as the demonstration of how a system for auditing might be useful. The process of describing health and development in detail, of fostering collaboration among parents, school personnel, medical caregivers, and other professionals, and of ensuring specialized attention when needed can enhance the quality of life for children now as well as in the future.

ACKNOWLEDGMENTS

The authors owe thanks to many colleagues in the planning, conduct and reporting of this study. Essential contributions were made by Dr. Frank Oberklaid, pediatric researcher; Margaret A. Hanson, nurse and medical coordinator; Marsha J. Rogers, diagnostic teacher; Barbara M. Murphy, prekindergarten coordinator; Dr. Mary Jane Yurchak, educational design; Dr. Elizabeth H. Nicol, editor; Kathleen Carspecken, graphics; Roxana Caminos and Shoshannah Fine, manuscript preparation.

REFERENCES

Baker, M. A., Lister, C., and Milhaus, R. 1976. Privacy and "Exceptional" Children: Issues of Recordkeeping Access and Confidentiality. Draft cited in: Doctors and Dollars are Not Enough: How To Improve Health Services for Children and Their Families. A report by the Children's Defense Fund of the Washington Research Project, Inc.

Dixon, M. S., 1974. EPSDT (Early and Periodic Screening, Diagnosis and Treatment Programs). Pediatrics 54:84–90.

Hauser-Cram, P., and Pierson, D. 1980. The BEEP Prekindergarten Curriculum. Unpublished manuscript. Brookline Early Education Project.

Holm, V. A., and McCartin, R. E. 1978. Interdisciplinary child development team: Team issues and training in interdisciplinariness. In: K. E. Allen, V. A. Holm, and R. L. Schiefelbusch (Eds.), Early Intervention: A Team Approach, pp. 99–122. University Park Press, Baltimore.

Levine, M. D., and Oberklaid, F. 1977. The Pediatric Extended Examination at Three (PEET). Brookline Early Education Project.

Levine, M. D., Palfrey, J., Lamb, G. A., Weisberg, H., and Bryk, A. 1977. Infants in a Public School System: The Indicators of Early Health and Educational Need. Pediatrics, 60:579–587.

Nicol, E. H. 1978. Recruiting Methods and Their Effectiveness. Brookline Early Education Project.

Oberklaid, F., Dworkin, P. H., and Levine, M. D. 1979. Developmental-behavioral dysfunction in preschool children: Descriptive analysis of a pediatric consultative model. Am. J. Dis. Child. 133:1126–1131.

Palfrey, J. S., Mervis, R. C., and Butler, J. A. 1978. New directions in the evaluation and education of handicapped children. New England J. Med. 298:819–824.

Sanazaro, P. J., Goldstein, R. L., Roberts, J. S., Maglott, D. B., and McAllister, J. W. 1972. Research and development in quality assurance. New England J. Med. 287:1125–1131.

Simeonsson, R. J., and Wiegerink, R. 1975. Accountability: A dilemma in infant intervention. Except. Child, 41:474–481.

Smith, M. S., and Bissell, J. S. 1970. Report analysis: The impact of Head Start. Harvard Educ. Rev. 40:51–104.

Starfield, B., and Barkowe, S. 1969. Physicians' recognition of complaints made by parents about their children's health. Pediatrics, 43:168–172.

Wise, H., Rubin, I., and Beckard, R. 1974. Making health teams work. Am. J. Dis. Child. 127:537–542.

Wolman, R., Yurchak, M. J., and Levine, M. D. 1980. Manual for the Longitudinal Study of Findings. Brookline Early Education Project.

Index